PIZZA COOKBOOK

The Ultimate Pizza Cookbook for Making Pizza at Home
(Discover 40+ Cheese-free Pizza Recipes)

Lucille Singleton

Published by Alex Howard

© **Lucille Singleton**
All Rights Reserved

Pizza Cookbook: The Ultimate Pizza Cookbook for Making Pizza at Home (Discover 40+ Cheese-free Pizza Recipes)

ISBN 978-1-990169-11-3

All rights reserved. No part of this guide may be reproduced in any form without permission in writing from the publisher except in the case of brief quotations embodied in critical articles or reviews.

Legal & Disclaimer

The information contained in this book is not designed to replace or take the place of any form of medicine or professional medical advice. The information in this book has been provided for educational and entertainment purposes only.

The information contained in this book has been compiled from sources deemed reliable, and it is accurate to the best of the Author's knowledge; however, the Author cannot guarantee its accuracy and validity and cannot be held liable for any errors or omissions. Changes are periodically made to this book. You must consult your doctor or get professional medical advice before using any of the suggested remedies, techniques, or information in this book.

Table of contents

PART 1 1

INTRODUCTION 2

PIZZA IN ITALY 3

Italian Pizza Dough 8
Sauces 11
Classic Pesto Sauce 12
Arugula Pesto Sauce 13
Marinara Sauce 14
Basil Pesto Sauce 16
Passata Pizza Sauce 17
Chef's Notes 18
Easy Pizza Sauce 19
Breakfast Pizza 20
Breakfast Spinach Pizza 22
French Bread Pizza 23
French Bread Pizza 23
Chef's Notes 25
Prosciutto Pizzas 27
Bacon Pizzas 29
Greek Pizzas 29
Tomato Olive Pizzas 30
Beef Pizzas 31
Mexican Taco Pizzas 32
Rustic French Bread Pizzas 33
Italian Pizzas 35
Classic Margherita Pizza 35
Chef's Notes 36
Parma Ham And Mozzarella Pizza 37
Napoletana Pizza 39
Prosciutto And Mozzarella Pizza 41
Rustic Cheese Pizza 42

Taleggio Pizza	43
Gorgonzola Cheese Pizza	44
Sicilian Pecorino Pizza	45
Sicilian Four Cheese Pizza	46
Roman Style Pizza	47
Caprese Pizza	49
Smoked Chorizo And Mozzarella Pizza	50
Vegan Pizza	52
Roasted Vegetable Pizza	53
Spinach And Chorizo Pizza	54
Potato And Parmigiano Cheese Pizza	55
Pesto And Prosciutto Pizza	57
Mediterranean Pizza	59
Artichoke And Garlic Pizza	60
Tomato And Mozzarella Pizza	62
Asparagus And Blue Cheese Pizza	64
Asparagus And Mozzarella Cheese Pizza	66
Pesto And Goat Cheese Pizza	68
Spinach And Mozzarella Cheese Pizza	69
Three Cheese Pizza	70
Chicken And Feta Cheese Pizza	72
Chef's Notes	73
Chorizo And Mushrooms Pizza	73
Pecorino And Mushrooms Pizza	74
Pepperoni And Gouda Cheese Pizza	76
Chicken and barbecue pizza	78
Hawaiian Pizza	79
Cheeseburger Pizza	81
Shrimp Garlic-Lemon Pizza	82
Shrimp Pesto Pizza	84
Green Pizza	85
Four Seasons Pizza	87
Anchovies And Capers Pizza	88
Zucchini And Chili Pizza	90
Pizza Fiorentina	91
PART 2	**93**

INTRODUCTION	94
HEALTHY VEGETARIAN PIZZAS	**95**
Stuffed Waffle Pizza	95
Two-Tomato Pizza	96
Basil Pesto & Tomato Pizza	98
Eggplant & Parmesan Cheese	100
Vegan Green Pizza	102
Chinese Pizza With Tofu	104
Barbecue Tofu Pizza	107
Tempeh Caesar Salad Pizza	110
Roasted Vegetables & Tempeh Pizza	113
Cauliflower Crust Pizza	116
Corn & Black Bean Pizza	118
Beans & Spicy Mango Pizza	121
Artichoke, Broccoli And Spinach Pesto Pizza	123
Chocolate Pizza	126
Raspberry Brie Pizza	128
MEAT LOVER PIZZAS	**130**
Chinese Chicken Hoisin Pizza	130
Chicken Garlic Pizza	133
Chicken, Bacon & Strawberry Pizza	135
Meatball Pizza	138
Pizza Cubano	140
Pepperoni & Cheese Tortilla Pizza	142
Avocado & Salmon Tortilla Pizza	144
Shrimp & Basil Pesto Pizza	146
Chicken & Bacon-Basil Pesto Pizza	148
Chicken-Broccoli Garlic Bread Pizza	151
Pepperoni Pizza	154
Sausage Pizza	156
California-Style Pizza Dough	157
California-Style Pizza Cheeses	159
Chicago-Style Deep Dish Pizza	162
Detroit-Style Pepperoni Pizzas	165

Grandma-Style Pizza	168
Grandma-Style Pizza Dough	170
New Haven-Style Clam Pizza	172
New York-Style Pizza	175
Pizza Bagels	177
St. Louis-Style Pizza	179
Neapolitan Pizza	181
Sicilian Pizza	184
Greek Pizza	186
Lahm Bi Ajeen Pizza	188
Margherita Pizza	190
Marinara Pizza	192

Part 1

Introduction

Italian cuisine is very regionally various on flavoring preferences, lifestyle, and language. However, all Italians are united by one — love to family and culinary traditions of the region. Traditions are their roots, is that they are. Like the plant. Like the tree. But the tree having roots yields absolutely different fruits. Two olives from one olive tree will never be identical, they are unique and therefore they are beautiful. This tree will yield a new harvest until has roots. As well with people, irrespective of nationality when Italians know and they honor their traditions, they can create something new. So, in the book are collected as the classical recipes checked decades and modern, in the author's interpretation of the Italian chefs.

Remember, any of these recipes can be made using store-bought dough with delicious results.

Pizza In Italy

Ahhh pizza, my favorite food, my passion! Fragrant, colorful and tasty, pizza is the most famous Italian gastronomic dish. And if, until a century ago, it could be enjoyed only in its birthplace Naples, today it can be enjoyed in every home kitchen. Of course, you can make pizza on your gas or charcoal grill. (Although, Italian pizzas always cook in a wood-fired oven. In fact, a pizzeria without one can't even, legally, call itself a pizzeria!).
Pizza is incredibly versatile: anything you have in the refrigerator you can turn into a pizza. The amazing aroma of freshly-baked pizza in all its variations at your home! Remember, Italian pizza is the best and most authentic when it's made with fresh, local ingredients.
I did some experimenting for 10 years, and here only winning combinations that expert pizzaiolos have developed over generations.

Vegetarian pizzas need not be limited. These recipes can be served in small slices with drinks before dinner or as a main course with a salad. Healthy eating has never been so delicious!

Traditionally, pizza and Italy didn't weren't always synonymous. In fact, a pizza wasn't even invented until the 19th century, when it started out as fast food on the streets of Naples. The classic Pizza Napoletana was like a dough with a tomato sauce (San Marzano tomatoes), oregano or basil herbs, a little garlic, sea salt, and extra virgin olive oil.

It's another pizza from Naples, called the Pizza Margherita. When Queen Margherita visited Naples in 1889, she was charmed by a local pizza baker (pizzaiolo) who had made, in her honor, a pizza with the colors of the new flag of Italy - red tomatoes, white Mozzarella cheese, and green fresh basil. Yep, you guessed it. It's now called the Pizza Margherita (or Margarita, on some menus).

Did you think about how it is correct to eat one of the most popular dishes of Italian cuisine – pizza?

About how it is correct to eat pizza, I will try to tell.

1. Traditional Neapolitan pizza is a dish on one person. Therefore everyone receives the pizza, it usually moves not cut. It is necessary to knife such a pizza table on 4 parts, helping yourself at the same time a fork. After that, it is possible to forget about a knife and a fork. When eating pizza it is necessary to fold hands one of four pieces double a stuffing inside.

2. "Purse" method. Traditional Neapolitan method of eating pizza. The whole pizza needs to be put four times a stuffing inside and to eat.

3. What to do with sides? Sides are a very important part of pizza, by the form it is possible to understand, the greatest pizzaiolo made pizza, or not really and whether he adhered to all subtleties of a compounding, at the preparation of pizza the Side has to be soft, with a pleasant aroma and literally melt in the mouth. But if it too crackling, pale, or on the contrary, burned slightly, shouldn't eat. And pizza too, it, most likely, is made incorrectly.

Interesting facts about pizza

In the United States, for example, about 3 billion portions of pizza annually are on sale, and it is the fact, as well as 20 others which you will find below. Bon appétit!

- As a rule, the adult uses 744 kcal with one pizza.
- 34 percent of fat in an organism of the typical American appear because of an excessive hobby for pizza.
- Men are the biggest fans of pizza. Women are in second place.
- Pizza can provide about 27 percent of the general energy demanded by an organism daily.
- The piece of cheese pizza contains on average from 220 to 370 kilocalories.
- We consume about 251.770.000 pounds of Pepperoni pizza every year.

- 93 percent of Americans ate pizza this month. It is a lot of cheese.
- About 3.000.000.000 portions of pizza are on sale annually in the United States.
- Each American annually eats about 46 pieces of pizza.
- In America, there are about 61 300 pizzerias.
- The largest pizza from ever made was 122 feet in size (8 feet in the diameter). Her preparation required about 9920 pounds of flour; 198 pounds of salt; 3968 pounds of cheese and 1984 pounds of tomato paste.
- Saturday nights are celebrated as the most popular time for eating pizza.
- Eating weekly pizza, you reduce the risk of a disease of gullet cancer.
- Trust or not, but mozzarella cheese makes about 80 percent of the production of the Italian cheeses in the USA.
- Pizza makes more than 10 percent of all sales of networks of public catering in the USA.
- The fastest cook in the world can make 14 full-size portions of pizza in 2 minutes and 35 seconds.
- 62 percent of the American population prefer toppings on a meat basis while other 38 percent give the vote in favor of vegetable pizza.
- 36 percent of Americans consider that pizza — an ideal breakfast.
- Today the most popular size of a pizza in the United States - 14 inches in the diameter.

Conversion chart
How to make the perfect pizza dough

Italian Pizza Dough using traditional type "00" flour. Why "00" flour? Italian type "00" or "doppio zero" flour has a higher protein level {12%} and gluten content. They label their flour in Italy by grind, not by protein or gluten content like we do here in the US. Type"00" is the finest grind of flour that is perfect for pizza, pasta, and Italian bread.
Maybe it just looks like usual pizza dough but, the texture and flavor of Italian Pizza Dough are completely different.
If you are chilling your pizza dough, you can also place each ball of dough in a plastic container instead of using a baking sheet.

Italian Pizza Dough

Prep Time: 3 hrs 15 mins

Ingredients
- 1 2/3 cup warm water 110 to 115 degrees
- ½ teaspoon active dry yeast
- 4 cups Type "00" Flour
- 2 teaspoons fine sea salt

Instructions
1. Sprinkle the yeast into a medium bowl with the warm water. That's the kind the yeast likes best. Stir until the yeast dissolves.
2. Place almost all of the flour on the table in the shape of a volcano.
3. Pour the yeast-and-sea-salt-and-warm-water mix, along with the other ingredients, into the "crater" of the volcano.
4. Knead everything together for 10 to 15 minutes until the dough is smooth and elastic, keeping your surface floured.
5. Grease up a bowl with some olive oil and put the dough inside. Turn the dough around so the top is slightly oiled.
6. Cover the bowl and put the dough aside to let it rest for at least four or five hours.

7. For those who want their pizza really authentic, optional. Make a cross on top of the dough with a knife. An old Italian tradition, this is seen as a way of "blessing the bread."
8. Preheat the oven to about 400°F.
9. Dump the dough out of the bowl and back onto the floured surface. Punch it down, getting rid of any bubbles. (Note: Now's the time to enlist a kid with more energy than they know what to do with!).
10. Divide the dough in half and let it rest for a few minutes.
11. Roll each section into a 12-inch disc. Now's your chance to decide how thick you want your pizza to be. Do you want it pizza Alta (Neapolitan-style) or pizza Bassa (Roman-style)? Just remember, your crust will puff up a little bit as it's baked!
12. Transfer the dough onto an oiled pizza pan or baking sheet.
13. Add tomato sauce, if you want a pizza Rossa (red pizza). Lots of pizzas in Italy are actually pizza Bianca, without tomato sauce, so don't feel like you have to! Brush the edges of the crust with a little bit of olive oil.
14. Bake each pizza for about 10 minutes, then add Mozzarella cheese (sliced or grated) on top, as well as any other ingredients.
15. Let the pizzas bake until the crust is browned and the cheese is melted. By lifting up the pizza to peek underneath, you can make sure the bottom has browned, too.

16. Remove your pizzas from the oven and, for a real Italian touch, garnish with a few basil leaves. And enjoy!

Sauces

Alfredo Sauce

Rich and creamy!

Serves 6-8
Prep time 10 minutes
Cook time 10 minutes
Total time 20 minutes

Ingredients

- ½ cup butter
- 1 pint heavy whipping cream (2 cups)
- 4 ounces cream cheese
- ½ teaspoon minced garlic
- 1 teaspoon garlic powder
- 1 teaspoon Italian seasoning
- ¼ teaspoon sea salt
- ¼ teaspoon ground black pepper
- 1 cup grated Parmesan cheese

How to make it

1. Melt butter in a medium saucepan, heavy whipping cream, and cream cheese. Cook over medium heat and whisk until melted. Add the minced garlic, garlic powder, Italian seasoning, sea salt, and black pepper. Continue to whisk until smooth. Add the grated parmesan cheese. Also, you can use Gruyere cheese or 1/2 cup shredded Mozzarella cheese.

2. Bring to a simmer and continue to cook for about 3-5 minutes or until it starts to thicken. Remove from the heat and serve.

Classic Pesto Sauce

Serves 8
Prep time 10 minutes
Cook time 10 minutes
Total time 10 minutes

Ingredients

- 4 cups basil
- 2-3 cloves garlic
- 1/4 cup pine nuts (or you can add pecans)
- 3/4 cup grated Parmesan cheese
- ½ teaspoon Kosher salt
- 3/4 - 1 cup extra virgin olive oil

How to make it

1. Add basil, garlic, pine nuts, Parmesan cheese, salt to the bowl of a food processor or high power blender.
2. Turn food processor on and begin slowly pouring olive oil through the chute of the machine, stopping to scrape down the sides of the bowl.
3. Store in the refrigerator for a few days or freeze in ice cube trays and then store in zip-top bags for a few months.

Arugula Pesto Sauce

Serves   1 cup
Prep time 5 minutes
Cook time 25 minutes
Total time 30 minutes

   Ingredients

- 4 cups arugula
- 2-3 cloves garlic
- ¼ cup walnuts
- ½ teaspoon sea salt
- ¾ - 1 cup extra virgin olive oil
- ¾ cup grated Parmesan cheese

How to make it

1. Add arugula, garlic, walnuts, and salt to the bowl of a food processor.
2. Turn food processor on and begin slowly pouring olive oil through the chute of the machine, stopping to scrape down the sides of the bowl.
3. Store in the refrigerator for a few days or freeze in ice cube trays and then store in zip-top bags for a few months.
4. Add Parmesan cheese to pesto when ready to use. Spread it onto a pizza and then top with chicken, spread it onto toasted bread with sliced tomatoes and basil. Delicious!

Marinara Sauce

You can add 2 tablespoons tomato paste for perfect color. Also, the sugar (1-2 tablespoons) to remove the "tinny" taste when using canned tomatoes.

Serves   ½ cup
Prep time 5 minutes
Cook time 25 minutes
Total time 30 minutes

Ingredients

- 2 tablespoons extra virgin olive oil
- 2 garlic cloves, minced
- ½ medium yellow onion diced
- ½ teaspoon sea salt
- ½ teaspoon fresh ground black pepper
- 1 32- ounce can crushed tomatoes (pureed)
- ½ teaspoon dried oregano
- ½ teaspoon thyme

How to make it

1. Heat the olive oil in a medium saucepan over medium-low heat. Add garlic and onions and cook until tender, about 5 minutes. Add the remaining ingredients and stir to combine. You can use an immersion blender, standard blender or even a food processor.
2. Simmer until slightly thickened, about 20 minutes.

3. Store in an airtight container in the refrigerator to keep for about 1 week.

Basil Pesto Sauce

Serves 2 cups
Prep time 5 minutes
Cook time 10 minutes
Total time 15 minutes

Ingredients

- 1 cup extra virgin olive oil
- 4 cups fresh basil leaves, packed
- 4 garlic cloves, smashed
- 1 cup Parmesan cheese, grated
- ½ cup pine nuts
- Sea salt & fresh ground black pepper to taste

How to make it

1. Place basil, garlic, Parmesan cheese, and pine nuts in the bowl of a food processor or immersion blender. Pulse until mixture is finely chopped.
2. With the machine running, gradually add the extra virgin olive oil until incorporated, about 10 minutes. Season with sea salt and black pepper to taste.
3. Store in an airtight container in the refrigerator to keep for about 1 week.

Passata Pizza Sauce

Serves   2 cups
Prep time 5 minutes
Cook time 35 minutes
Total time 40 minutes

   Ingredients
- 1/4 cup extra virgin olive oil
- ½ medium onion, finely diced
- 2 cloves garlic minced
- 1/4 teaspoon cayenne pepper
- 1 teaspoon dried oregano
- 1 28-ounce can crushed tomatoes
- 1 6-ounce can tomato paste
- 1 teaspoon sea salt
- 1 teaspoon granulated sugar
- 1 teaspoon ground black pepper
- 2 teaspoons chopped fresh oregano

How to make it

1.   Drizzle olive oil into a 3-quart saucepan over medium heat. Add onions and cook until translucent and tender, about 3 minutes. Stir in garlic, cayenne pepper, and dried oregano. Cook for about 1 minute to release flavors.

2.   Pour in tomatoes, tomato paste, and add sea salt, sugar, and black pepper. Stir well to combine. Add fresh oregano. Reduce heat to low-medium and simmer for about 30 minutes, stirring often to prevent any sticking or burning.

3.   Remove from heat and use immediately or allow to cool before storing in an airtight container for up to one week.

Chef's Notes

If your pizza sauce seems a bit chunky, you can use an immersion blender or regular blender to make it rich and creamy. Make this pizza sauce up to a week before and you'll always be ready for friends!

Easy Pizza Sauce

Serves 8
Prep time 5 minutes
Cook time 5 minutes
Total time 5 minutes

Ingredients

- 6 oz tomato Passata sauce
- 5 tablespoons extra virgin olive oil
- 2 cloves garlic, minced
- Sea salt and freshly ground black pepper to taste
- ½ tablespoon dried oregano
- ½ tablespoon dried basil
- ½ teaspoon dried rosemary, crushed
- 10 fl oz water (or less)

How to make it

1. Mix together the tomato Passata and extra virgin olive oil. Mix well. Add garlic, salt, and pepper to taste, oregano, basil, and rosemary. Also, you can add Italian seasoning to taste. Mix well and gradually add the water, stopping when you've reached your desired consistency.
2. Let stand for several hours to let the flavors blend. No cooking necessary just spread on the pizza base.

Breakfast Pizza

Breakfast Bacon Pizza
Serves   6
Prep time 2 hours
Cook time 40 minutes
Total time 2 hours, 40 minutes

   Ingredients
- 1 pizza dough
- ½ pound bulk sausage
- 6 slices uncured thick-cut bacon (cooked, cut into pieces)
- 6 large eggs
- 1 cup shredded Cheddar cheese
- 4 tablespoons all-purpose flour
- 1 cup milk (you can use coconut milk)
- green onions (garnish)
- corn meal (to dust pizza peel)

How to make it

1. Place a baking stone in the cold oven, and heat oven to 500 degrees for 1 hour.
2. Make your pizza dough or remove from refrigerator and allow to sit at room temperature.
3. Cook bacon, set aside.

4. Cook sausage. Drain and reserve fat. Heat 4 tablespoons of fat in skillet, add 4 tablespoons of flour. Whisk together to create a roux.
5. Add milk, use a whisk to combine.
6. Heat until gravy thickens, set aside. Scramble the eggs, set aside.
7. Dust pizza peel or flat baking sheet with cornmeal. Place pizza dough on peel.
8. Spread half of the gravy on top of dough. Sprinkle sausage over gravy.
9. Using kitchen shears, cut bacon into chunks and sprinkle on top of the pizza.
10. Add the scrambled eggs. Sprinkle grated cheese on top.
11. Slide onto the preheated pizza peel and bake 8-10 minutes, or until cheese has melted and crust is golden brown.
12. Garnish with green onions. Repeat with the second pizza.

Breakfast Spinach Pizza

Serves 4
Cook time 25 minutes
Total time 50 minutes

Ingredients

- 4 slices bacon
- 6 ounces baby spinach leaves
- 3 cloves garlic, thinly sliced
- 1 tablespoon plain yellow cornmeal
- 12 ounces store-bought pizza dough, at room temperature
- 4 large eggs
- 6 ounces Fontina cheese, grated (1½ cups)

How to make it

1. Heat oven to 450°F. Cook bacon in a 10-inch ovenproof skillet (preferably cast iron) over medium heat until crisp, 12 to 15 minutes. Remove bacon from pan, then add the spinach and garlic. Cook, stirring occasionally, until the spinach wilts, 4 minutes. Set mixture aside and wipe out skillet.

2. Sprinkle cornmeal into skillet. Add dough, pressing it gently until it covers the bottom and reaches 1 inch up the sides of the skillet. Place over medium heat and cook for 8 minutes, until the bottom of the dough begins to brown. As the dough cooks, top with reserved bacon, spinach, eggs, and Fontina cheese.

3. Transfer the skillet to the oven and bake on bottom rack until the crust is golden, eggs are set, and cheese begins to brown, 10-15 minutes. Let rest 5 minutes before slicing.

French Bread Pizza

Great tasting French bread pizza perfect for that quick evening meal or a party. And at only 20 minutes!

Forget ordering out, making your own personal French bread pizzas is customizable, inexpensive, and delicious!

French Bread Pizza

Serves 6-8
Prep time 5 minutes
Cook time 20 minutes
Total time 25 minutes

Ingredients

- 1 pound loaf soft French bread, split in thirds lengthwise
- 8 tablespoons (1 stick) unsalted butter
- 4 cloves garlic, finely chopped
- 3 tablespoons chopped fresh flat-leaf parsley leaves
- ¾ teaspoon dried oregano

- 1¼ teaspoons Kosher salt, divided
- 1 28-oz. can diced tomatoes, drained
- 2 tablespoons extra virgin olive oil
- ½ teaspoon crushed red pepper flakes (optional)
- Freshly ground black pepper, to taste
- 12 ounces Mozzarella cheese, grated
- 3 ounces Parmesan cheese, grated

How to make it

1. Heat oven to 425°F. Cut your bread into the size you want your pizzas. Place bread cut side up on a lightly oiled baking sheet.

2. Melt the butter in a small saucepan over medium heat. Add the garlic and cook, stirring often, until fragrant, 1 to 2 minutes; let cool slightly. Add the parsley, oregano, and ½ teaspoon salt. Brush the butter mixture onto the bread. Bake until the edges of the bread are crisp, 6-7 minutes. Remove from the oven.

3. Meanwhile, combine the tomatoes, olive oil, red pepper flakes, several grinds black pepper and remaining ¾ teaspoon salt in a blender or food processor and pulse until smooth.

4. Spread tomato sauce on the toasted bread. Top with Mozzarella and Parmesan cheese. Broil on high until the cheese is golden brown and bubbly, 6-7 minutes. Every oven is different but mine took between 10 and 15 minutes.

Chef's Notes

You can make these pizzas on any type of French bread. But you need a nice French bread. Because the quality of the bread will determine your taste. Also, some French bread has a harder crust.

Three Cheese Pizzas

Add 1 oz. Asiago per third before baking

Pepperoni Pizzas

Add 1 cup chopped pepperoni per third before baking

Margherita Pizzas

Add fresh basil after baking

Ingredients for French bread pizzas

Vegan Pizzas

- 4 roasted red peppers
- Sliced tomatoes
- One 12-ounce jar olives
- Sliced mushrooms

- Parmesan cheese
- 2 tablespoons extra virgin olive oil
- Sea salt and freshly ground black pepper

Prosciutto Pizzas

- Prosciutto slices
- Bleu cheese
- Mozzarella cheese
- 1 cup Sauce Alfredo

Provance Pizzas

- Ham slices
- Bleu cheese
- Sliced tomatoes
- 1 cup Sauce Alfredo

Meetzzas Pizzas

- Ham slices
- Pepperoni slices
- Chorizo slices
- Mozzarella cheese
- Parmesan cheese
- 1 cup Sauce BBQ or Marinara

Pepperoni Pizzas

- Pepperoni slices
- Mozzarella cheese
- Sliced tomatoes
- 1 cup Pizza Sauce or Marinara

Chicken and Pineapple Pizzas

- Pineapple chunks
- Mozzarella cheese

- Chicken grilled
- 1 cup Passata Sauce or Marinara, optional

Bacon Pizzas

- bacon slices, halved
- canned pineapple chunks

Greek Pizzas

- 3 tablespoons extra virgin olive oil
- Sea salt and freshly ground black pepper
- One jar olives, chopped
- 6 ounces crumbled Feta cheese
- 3 ripe tomatoes, diced rough
- ½ cucumber, seeded and diced
- ½ bunch fresh parsley, chopped

How to make it

1. Leave off the sauce and brush the sliced rolls with 1 tablespoon of the olive oil; sprinkle with sea salt and ground black pepper. Bake on middle rack until nicely browned. About 10 minutes.

2. While the pizzas are baking, toss together the olives, Feta cheese, tomatoes, cucumbers, parsley, the remaining 2 tablespoons olive oil and sea salt and black pepper to taste in a small bowl. Add to top the cooked pizzas the chopped Greek salad.

Tomato Olive Pizzas

- Cherry tomatoes, for topping
- One 12-ounce jar olives
- 2 tablespoons extra virgin olive oil
- Kosher salt and freshly ground black pepper
- ½ bunch fresh basil
- 1 cup Pesto sauce

How to make it

Drizzle with the olive oil and sprinkle with salt and black pepper. Bake on middle rack until nicely browned. About 10 minutes. Top the cooked pizzas with fresh basil leaves.

Beef Pizzas

- Extra virgin olive oil
- 1 pound ground beef
- 1 teaspoon red pepper flakes
- Kosher salt and freshly ground black pepper
- Cherry tomatoes, for topping

How to make it

1. Heat the olive oil in a skillet over medium-high heat.
2. Add the ground beef, red pepper flakes and kosher salt and ground black pepper and saute until the beef is no longer pink.
3. Top the rolls with the sauteed ground beef and fresh cherry tomatoes.
4. Bake for 8-10 minutes.

Mexican Taco Pizzas

- 8 ounces grated Mexican cheese
- 1 pound browned ground beef
- Chopped fresh lettuce, for topping
- Diced tomatoes, for topping
- 3 cloves garlic, finely chopped
- Sea alt and freshly ground black pepper

How to make it

Top with the Mexican cheese and ground beef and garlic, then bake for 5-6 minutes, or until lightly browned. You can use Gruyère cheese or Fontina also. If Top the cooked pizzas with the chopped lettuce and tomatoes.

Rustic French Bread Pizzas

Serves   4
Prep time 10 minutes
Cook time 25 minutes
Total time 35 minutes

Ingredients

- 1 (2 foot long) loaf French bread
- 1 pound sweet Italian sausage
- 1 tablespoon extra virgin olive oil
- 1 small red bell pepper, seeded and chopped
- 1 small onion, chopped
- 2 large cloves garlic, chopped
- 1 package frozen chopped spinach defrosted and squeezed dry
- Sea alt and black pepper, to your taste
- 1 ½ cups part skim Ricotta cheese
- ½ cup grated Parmesan cheese
- ½ pound sweet soppressata, from the deli, sliced thick, chopped
- ½ stick pepperoni, chopped
- 10 ounces shredded Mozzarella cheese
- 10 ounces shredded Provolone cheese
- 1 teaspoon dried oregano
- 1 teaspoon crushed red pepper flake

How to make it

1. Preheat oven to 425º F.

2. Split bread lengthwise and hollow it out. Cut in half across, making 4 shells for pizzas.

3. Heat a skillet over medium-high flame and brown sausage in olive oil. Brown and crumble sausage. Add red bell pepper, onion, and garlic. Cook 3 to 5 minutes, add spinach. Remove mixture from heat and season with a pinch of salt and black pepper, to your taste.

4. Transfer to a bowl. Combine sausage and veggies with ricotta, Parmesan, soppressata and pepperoni. Fill bread shells and top with mounded Mozzarella and Provolone cheeses. Place in hot oven on cookie sheet and bake until cheese melts and bubbles and bread are super crisp about 10 to 12 minutes.

5. Top pizzas with oregano and hot pepper flakes.

6. Serve immediately, or snack all night!

Italian Pizzas

Classic Margherita Pizza

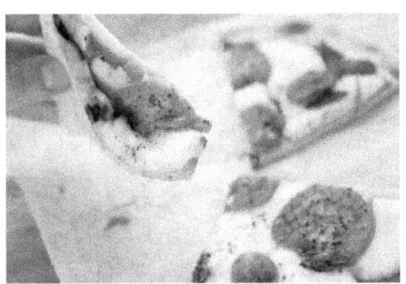

Serves   8
Prep time 5 minutes
Cook time 15 minutes
Total time 20 minutes

   Ingredients
- 1 pizza dough
- 1 cup Passata sauce
- 5 ½ oz Mozzarella cheese, drained and cut into little cubes
- 4 tablespoons extra virgin olive oil
- 8 fresh basil leaves
- sea salt and black pepper to taste

How to make it

1. Preheat the oven to 450º F.
2. Place the pizza dough on the oiled baking trays.
3. Spread the Passata sauce evenly over the top of the pizza.
4. Season with sea salt and black pepper.
5. Top with Mozzarella cheese and drizzle with 2 tablespoons of olive oil.
6. Cook in the middle of the oven for 15 minutes until golden brown.
7. Two minutes before the end of the cooking, scatter over the basil leaves and continue to cook.

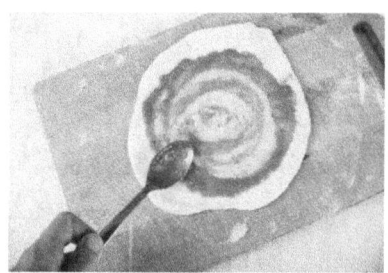

Chef's Notes

A traditional pizza Margherita of Naples, complete with the thick crust. If you like it hot, you can always drizzle a little chili oil on top before serving.

Parma Ham And Mozzarella Pizza

Serves   4
Prep time 5 minutes
Cook time 15 minutes
Total time 20 minutes

   Ingredients
- 1 pizza dough
- 2 tablespoons extra virgin olive oil
- 1 cup puréed tomatoes (or Passata sauce)
- 8 oz Mozzarella Buffalo cheese, drained and cut into little cubes
- 1 onion, chopped
- 2 cloves garlic
- 2 oz arugula leaves
- 1 cup Parma ham, sliced
- 4 figs
- 4 teaspoons sugar
- Sea salt and black pepper to taste

How to make it

1.   Preheat the oven to 355º F.

2.   For the sauce, finely diced garlic and onion. Then sauté the onion and garlic in olive oil until translucent.

3.   Pour in the pureed tomatoes and season with sugar and a pinch of salt and fresh ground black pepper. Leave the sauce to reduce for approx. 5 – 7 min. on low heat.

4. Roll out the thin dough and place on a lined baking tray.

5. Spread the Passata sauce evenly on the dough.

6. Sliced Mozzarella cheese and lay it evenly across the pizza.

7. Bake the pizza in a preheated oven at 355°F for 20 - 25 minutes, until golden brown.

8. Two minutes before the end of the cooking, cover with fresh arugula leaves and Parma ham. Quarter figs and distribute over the pizza.

9. Enjoy served warm.

Napoletana Pizza

Serves 4
Prep time 15 minutes
Cook time 10 minutes
Total time 25 minutes

Ingredients

- 1 pizza dough
- 2 tablespoons extra virgin olive oil
- 1 small onion, finely chopped
- 2 garlic cloves, crushed
- 2 cans chopped tomatoes
- ½ tablespoon caster sugar
- 1 handful of fresh basil leaves, torn into pieces
- 5½ oz Mozzarella cheese, thinly sliced
- 8 anchovy fillets, halved lengthways
- 8 black olives, stoned and halved
- Sea salt and black pepper

How to make it

1. Preheat the oven to 425º F.
2. Heat the extra virgin olive oil in a saucepan, add the onion and garlic, and cook gently, stirring, for 3 minutes or until softened. Add the tomatoes with their juice, the sugar, and salt and pepper to taste, and bring to the boil. Leave the mixture to bubble, stirring frequently, until reduced by about half to

make a thick sauce. Remove from the heat and leave to cool.

3. Stir the basil into the tomato sauce. Spread the sauce over the pizza dough to within ½ in of the edge. Arrange the Mozzarella cheese, anchovies and olives over the top.
4. Bake the pizza for 20–25 minutes or until the crust has risen and is golden and the cheese has melted.

Prosciutto And Mozzarella Pizza

Serves   4
Prep time 5 minutes
Cook time 20 minutes
Total time 25 minutes

Ingredients

- 1 pizza dough
- 2 tablespoons extra virgin olive oil
- 8 oz grated Mozzarella cheese
- 4 oz prosciutto, sliced
- 3 ½ oz tomatoes
- Sea salt to taste

How to make it

1. Preheat the oven to 400º F.
2. Place the pizza dough on a floured pizza peel, one at a time. Place the sliced tomatoes, prosciutto, grated Mozzarella cheese.
3. Add olive oil and sea salt on pizza dough.
4. Bake the pizza for 20 minutes or until the cheese has melted.

Rustic Cheese Pizza

Serves 4
Prep time 5 minutes
Cook time 30 minutes
Total time 35 minutes

Ingredients
- 1 pizza dough
- ½ cup Ricotta cheese
- 1 ¼ cups Provolone cheese
- ¼ cup Parmigiano Reggiano cheese, grated
- 3 eggs
- 3 ½ oz prosciutto, sliced
- 1 ¾ oz salami, sliced
- Sea salt and black pepper

How to make it

1. Preheat the oven to 375º F.
2. Mixed egg yolks, sea salt, black pepper, and all cheeses.
3. Place the pizza dough on a floured pizza peel.
4. Cover with the sliced prosciutto and three kinds of cheese with eggs.
5. Bake the pizza for 20 minutes or until the cheese has melted.

Taleggio Pizza

Serves 4
Prep time 10 minutes
Cook time 20 minutes
Total time 30 minutes

Ingredients

- 1 pizza dough
- 7 oz Taleggio cheese, sliced
- 8 walnut kernels
- 4 tablespoons extra virgin olive oil
- Sea salt to taste

How to make it

1. Preheat the oven to 400º F.
2. Place the pizza dough on a floured pizza peel, one at a time.
3. Add the toppings (all except for the walnuts) and place on a pizza stone in a hot oven for 20 minutes.
4. Top with walnuts sprinkled to serve.

Gorgonzola Cheese Pizza

Serves   4
Prep time 10 minutes
Cook time 20 minutes
Total time 30 minutes

　　Ingredients

- 1 pizza dough
- 1 cup Gorgonzola cheese, sliced
- ½ cup black olives, pitted
- 3 tablespoons extra virgin olive oil
- Sea salt to taste

How to make it

1. Preheat the oven to 400º F.
2. Place the pizza dough on a floured pizza peel, one at a time.
3. Cover dough with extra-virgin olive oil and sprinkle with Gorgonzola cheese and olives.
4. Place on a pizza stone in a hot oven for 20 minutes.

Sicilian Pecorino Pizza

Serves 8
Prep time 10 minutes
Cook time 20 minutes
Total time 30 minutes

Ingredients

- 1 pizza dough
- 3 ½ oz Pecorino cheese, grated
- 3 ½ oz salami
- 6 tablespoons Passata Sauce
- 3 tablespoons extra virgin olive oil
- Sea salt to taste

How to make it

1. Preheat the oven to 400º F.
2. Place pizza dough on a greased pizza tray.
3. Cover dough with extra virgin olive oil and add tomato sauce.
4. Sprinkle with Pecorino cheese.
5. Place salami over the pizza and season sea salt to taste.
6. Bake in preheated oven about 20 minutes.

Sicilian Four Cheese Pizza

Serves   8
Prep time 10 minutes
Cook time 20 minutes
Total time 30 minutes

Ingredients

- 1 pizza dough
- 3 oz Provolone cheese
- 3 oz Parmigiano Reggiano cheese, thinly sliced
- 3 oz Gruyere, thinly sliced
- 3 oz Pecorino cheese, thinly sliced
- 5 tablespoons extra virgin olive oil
- Sea salt to taste

How to make it

1. Preheat the oven to 400º F.
2. Place pizza dough on a greased pizza tray.
3. Cover dough with extra virgin olive oil and add all cheeses.
4. Season sea salt to taste.
5. Bake in preheated oven about 20 minutes.

Roman Style Pizza

Serves   8
Prep time 10 minutes
Cook time 20 minutes
Total time 30 minutes

Ingredients

- 1 pizza dough
- ¼ cup Parmesan cheese, grated
- 3 onions, sliced
- 4 tablespoons extra virgin olive oil
- 2 tablespoons unsalted butter
- 16 olives, pitted
- 12 anchovy fillets, rinsed under cold running water, drained
- 1 teaspoon fresh thyme, chopped
- Sea salt to taste

How to make it

1. Preheat the oven to 450º F.
2. Slice onions very thinly. In a large skillet heat olive oil and butter over medium heat. Add onions. Cook for 15-20 minutes, stirring occasionally until onions are soft. Then add sea salt and continue to cook 15-25 minutes until onions are translucent and very soft. When onions are toffee-colored, transfer them to a bowl.
3. Place pizza dough on a baking sheet.

4. Spread caramelized onions evenly over the surface of the dough, leaving a 1" border all around.

5. Sprinkle with fresh thyme and Parmesan cheese.

6. Criss-cross two anchovy halves to mark each of 12 pieces (one criss-cross per piece) and add olives (the number of anchovies and olives may be increased if you prefer).

7. Bake in preheated oven for 20 to 25 minutes.

Caprese Pizza

Serves 8
Prep time 10 minutes
Cook time 15 minutes
Total time 25 minutes

Ingredients

- 1 pizza dough
- ¼ cup Parmesan cheese, grated
- ½ cup Bocconcini cheese (or Goat cheese)
- ½ cup Passata sauce (or Marinara)
- ½ teaspoon fresh thyme, chopped
- ½ teaspoon oregano, chopped
- ¼ cup fresh basil leaves, shredded

How to make it

1. Preheat the oven to 450º F.
2. Place pizza dough on a baking sheet.
3. Spread crust with enough tomato sauce to coat evenly.
4. Sprinkle with Parmesan cheese and Bocconcini cheese.
5. Add fresh basil leaves, fresh thyme, and oregano.
6. Bake in preheated oven for 10 to 15 minutes.

Smoked Chorizo And Mozzarella Pizza

Serves 4
Prep time 15 minutes
Cook time 10 minutes
Total time 25 minutes

Ingredients

- 1 pizza dough
- 5 cloves garlic
- 2 sliced tomatoes
- 8 oz grated Mozzarella cheese
- ½ cup grated Cheddar cheese
- 4 fl.oz smoked chorizo
- 1 red pepper
- 2 tablespoons extra virgin olive oil

How to make it

1. Preheat the oven to 425º F.
2. Very finely slice the garlic and add to tomatoes and olive oil. Alternately you can blitz all the ingredients in a mini blender.
3. Spread sauce over the prepared pizza dough, then ½ cup Mozzarella cheese.
4. Top with smoked chorizo slices and sliced red pepper.
5. Bake in the oven, until the cheese, is melted and golden, for 8 minutes.

Vegan Pizza

Serves 4
Prep time 15 minutes
Cook time 10 minutes
Total time 25 minutes

Ingredients

- 1 pizza dough
- 4 tablespoons extra virgin olive oil
- 8 tablespoons Passata Sauce
- 2 small red onions, chopped
- 2 garlic cloves, crushed
- 1 oz Parmesan cheese
- 1 yellow pepper
- 1 red pepper
- ½ small aubergine, 5½ oz
- 8 anchovy fillets, halved lengthways
- 8 black olives, stoned and halved
- Sea salt and black pepper

How to make it

1. Toss the vegetables with olive oil in a roasting tin, then roast in an oven preheated to 425º F for 25 minutes or until soft. Arrange the vegetables on the Italian tomato sauce in place of the Mozzarella cheese and anchovies, and scatter over the olives.
2. After baking, sprinkle with 1 oz Parmesan cheese.

Roasted Vegetable Pizza

Serves   6
Prep time 10 minutes
Cook time 25 minutes
Total time 35 minutes

Ingredients

- 1 pizza dough
- 1 tablespoon extra virgin olive oil
- 1 small onion, thinly sliced
- 3 garlic cloves, minced
- 1 zucchini, sliced
- 2 cups Mozzarella cheese, shredded
- 1 small yellow squash, sliced
- 1 red pepper
- 1 tablespoon fresh thyme
- Sea salt to taste

How to make it

1. Preheat the oven to 425º F.
2. Coat pizza pan with 1 teaspoon of olive oil.
3. Spread out pizza dough on the pan and build up edges to form a crust. Bake for 6 to 7 minutes.
4. Remove crust from oven then preheat the oven to 500° F.
5. To roast the vegetables, combine 1 teaspoon extra virgin olive oil, fresh thyme, sea salt, garlic, red pepper, zucchini, squash, and onion in a baking dish and bake

for 7 minutes. Stir the vegetables and bake for another 7 minutes. When done, reduce oven to 425°F.

6. Sprinkle 1 cup Mozzarella cheese over the pizza crust. Spread the vegetables over the cheese and sprinkle with the remaining cheese.

7. Bake in preheated oven for 12 to 15 minutes.

Spinach And Chorizo Pizza

Serves 4
Prep time 15 minutes
Cook time 10 minutes
Total time 25 minutes

   Ingredients
- 1 pizza dough
- 4 tablespoons extra virgin olive oil
- 8 tablespoons Passata Sauce
- 7 oz baby spinach leaves
- 2 oz Mozzarella cheese
- 7 oz sliced chestnut mushrooms
- ½ oz butter
- 8 anchovy fillets, halved lengthways
- 8 black olives, stoned and halved
- 2 tablespoons pine nuts
- 1 oz chorizo sausage, thinly sliced

How to make it

1. Put baby spinach leaves in a saucepan, cover and cook for 1–2 minutes or until just wilted.

2. Fry sliced chestnut mushrooms in ½ oz butter until their liquid has evaporated and they are just starting to color.

3. Arrange the spinach leaves and mushrooms on the Italian tomato sauce in place of the Mozzarella cheese, anchovies and black olives.

4. Scatter over 1 oz thinly sliced chorizo sausage and pine nuts, then rise and bake in preheated oven about 10 minutes.

Potato And Parmigiano Cheese Pizza

Serves 8
Prep time 15 minutes
Cook time 15 minutes
Total time 30 minutes

Ingredients

- 1 pizza dough
- 1 large potato, peeled and diced into small cubes
- 2 tablespoons basil Pesto sauce
- 1 yellow pepper cut into small cubes
- 1 red pepper cut into small cubes
- 1 red onion cut into cubes
- 2 handfuls of fresh baby spinach leaves
- 4 oz grated Mozzarella cheese
- 4 oz grated Parmigiano cheese
- ½ cup Goat cheese
- 2 tablespoons extra virgin olive oil

- Sea salt and black pepper to taste

How to make it

1. Preheat oven to 425º F.
2. Place pizza dough on a greased pizza tray.
3. Cover dough with extra-virgin olive oil and sprinkle with Parmigiano and Mozzarella cheese.
4. In a frying pan, heat olive oil and saute all veggies (except baby spinach) for 10 - 12 minutes.
5. Place veggies in a large bowl and add spinach leaves and toss until well mixed. Spinach will wilt and become soft.
6. Then add 2 heaping tablespoons of Pesto sauce and salt and pepper to taste to a bowl and mix well.
7. Distribute stirfry evenly over pizza dough and crumble Goat cheese over entire pizza.
8. Bake in preheated oven about 20 minutes.

Pesto And Prosciutto Pizza

Serves   8
Prep time 15 minutes
Cook time 10 minutes
Total time 25 minutes

    Ingredients
- 1 pizza dough
- 8 tablespoons Pesto Sauce
- 4 oz Mozzarella cheese
- 2 fl.oz prosciutto (chopped, if desired)
- 4 tablespoons chopped fresh parsley
- 3 tablespoons chopped fresh basil
- 3 tablespoons grated Parmesan cheese

How to make it

1. Preheat oven to 425º F.

2. Spread the Pesto sauce evenly on the pizza dough. Arrange Mozzarella cheese over the Pesto, scatter prosciutto over the Mozzarella cheese. Sprinkle pizza with the fresh parsley, fresh basil, and grated Parmesan cheese.

3. Bake in preheated oven about 10 minutes.

Mediterranean Pizza

Olives, artichokes, tomatoes with Feta cheese are the perfect toppings for a Greek style pizza.

Serves 8
Prep time 10 minutes
Cook time 20 minutes
Total time 30 minutes

Ingredients

- 1 pizza dough
- 2 cups Mozzarella cheese, grated
- ¼ cup Feta cheese, crumbled
- 2 small jars marinated artichoke hearts
- 1 cup black olives, chopped
- 1 cup cherry tomatoes, halved
- 1 teaspoon oregano, dried
- ½ teaspoon thyme, dried
- 2 tablespoons fresh basil leaves, chopped
- 1 tablespoon extra virgin olive oil

How to make it

1. Preheat the oven to 425º F.
2. Drain artichokes, reserving marinade. Chop artichokes and set aside.
3. Place pizza dough on a baking sheet. Lightly brush the dough with olive oil.
4. Sprinkle with chopped basil, oregano, and thyme.

5. Add 1 cup Mozzarella cheese, artichoke hearts, tomatoes, olives, and Feta cheese. Sprinkle with remaining cheese.

6. Bake for 20-25 minutes or until cheese is lightly browned.

Artichoke And Garlic Pizza

Easy and delicious homemade pizza with sauce, artichoke hearts, tomatoes, garlic and Cheddar cheese.

Serves   8
Prep time 15 minutes
Cook time 20 minutes
Total time 35 minutes

Ingredients

- 1 pizza dough
- ¾ cup Italian Passata sauce
- 1 cup marinated artichoke hearts, drained, liquid reserved
- 1 medium tomato, halved and sliced
- 2 cloves garlic, minced
- 1 cup grated Monterey Jack and Cheddar cheese

How to make it

1. Preheat the oven to 425º F. Prepare pizza dough according to the recipe. Place on a pizza tin.

2. Pour the liquid from the artichokes into a small frying pan, and bring to the boil over medium heat. Cook for 1 minute, or until the liquid is almost gone. Add garlic, and cook, stirring, for less than a minute. Add artichoke hearts, stir to coat with garlic flavor, then remove from heat, and set aside.

3. Spread sauce over the prepared pizza dough. Sprinkle with cheese, then place the artichoke hearts and garlic over the cheese. Arrange tomato slices evenly over the top.

4. Bake for 20 minutes in the preheated oven, until pizza is golden and cheese is melted.

Tomato And Mozzarella Pizza

Serves 8
Prep time 15 minutes
Cook time 20 minutes
Total time 35 minutes

Ingredients

- 1 pizza dough
- 2 cloves of garlic
- 1 tablespoon extra virgin olive oil
- 1 cup tinned chopped tomatoes
- Sea salt and black pepper to taste
- 1 teaspoon dried oregano
- 1 cup grated Mozzarella cheese
- 1 cup fresh basil leaves

How to make it

1. Prepare pizza dough and place on a pizza tin.
2. Preheat the oven to 425º F.
3. In the meantime, make the sauce. Mince garlic and fry in olive oil until soft. Add tomatoes, sea salt, and black pepper to taste. Sprinkle with oregano and simmer on low heat until thickened, 15 to 20 minutes. Let cool.
4. Spoon sauce on top of the pizza.
5. Layer sliced Mozzarella cheese and fresh basil leaves on top.
6. Bake pizza for 10 minutes until Mozzarella cheese is bubbly.

Asparagus And Blue Cheese Pizza

You can use any sort of Blue cheese you prefer.

Serves 6
Prep time 10 minutes
Cook time 20 minutes
Total time 30 minutes

Ingredients

- pizza dough
- 1 cup asparagus, trimmed and snapped into pieces
- 1 teaspoon extra virgin olive oil, or as needed
- Sea salt and ground black pepper
- ½ cup Passata tomato sauce
- ½ cup crumbled Blue cheese

How to make it

1. Preheat the oven to 400º F.

2. Place asparagus on a baking tray. Drizzle with olive oil and sprinkle with sea salt and black pepper.

3. Bake the asparagus in the preheated oven 8 to 10 minutes.

4. While asparagus is baking, spread the Passata sauce over the pizza dough. Distribute asparagus pieces and crumbles of Blue cheese over the pizza.

5. Return pizza to center rack of preheated oven.

6. Bake until the cheese is melted and bubbling, 8 to 10 minutes.

Asparagus And Mozzarella Cheese Pizza

A great way to enjoy asparagus when in season and to get kids to eat! You can add Pesto sauce too and as much cheese or tomatoes as you want. This is a delicious pizza without Italian Passata sauce.

Serves 8
Prep time 15 minutes
Cook time 25 minutes
Total time 40 minutes

Ingredients

- 1 pizza dough
- 5 bacon rashers
- 1 cup grated Mozzarella cheese
- ½ ounces chopped fresh asparagus
- ½ ounces halved cherry tomatoes
- 9 ounces goat cheese
- 1 teaspoon red chili flakes
- ground black pepper to taste

How to make it

1. Preheat the oven to 425º F.

2. Place bacon in a frying pan over medium-high heat. Cook for a few minutes, but do not cook until crisp. Remove to kitchen roll and set aside.

3. Place the pizza dough on a pizza tin. Top with Mozzarella cheese, bacon pieces, asparagus, and cherry tomatoes. Dot with Goat cheese, then season with red chili flakes and pepper.

4. Bake for 15 to 20 minutes in the preheated oven.

Pesto And Goat Cheese Pizza

The herbed Goat cheese is great with all the flavors! Also, you can add fresh ground pepper before chopping it up as the topping to taste.

Serves 8
Prep time 10 minutes
Cook time 10 minutes
Total time 20 minutes

Ingredients

- 1 pizza dough
- 1/3 cup Pesto sauce
- 3 sliced plum tomatoes
- 8 ounces herbed Goat cheese
- 2 thinly sliced cloves garlic
- 1 cup of fresh arugula
- 2 teaspoons extra virgin olive oil
- some lemon juice for arugula

How to make it

1. Preheat the oven to 425º F.

2. Add Pesto sauce onto the center of the pizza dough, and spread toward the outer edges. Cut the Goat cheese into thin coins and spread or crumble across the pizza. Arrange tomato slices over Goat cheese. Sprinkle with garlic. Brush the pizza edges lightly with extra virgin olive oil.

3. Place pizza directly on preheated oven rack. Bake for 5 to 10 minutes or until the pizza edges are golden.

4. After taking the pizza out of the oven, allow cooling for a few minutes so that the cheese has time to set. After a couple of minutes, cover the pizza with a cup of arugula with some lemon juice and olive oil. Cut, serve and enjoy!

Spinach And Mozzarella Cheese Pizza

Delicious!
Serves   8
Prep time 15 minutes
Cook time 20 minutes
Total time 35 minutes

Ingredients

- 1 pizza dough
- ¼ cup melted butter
- 1 tablespoon extra virgin olive oil
- 3 tablespoons minced garlic
- 2 tablespoons sun-dried tomatoes sauce
- 1 teaspoon dried basil leaves
- 1 teaspoon dried oregano
- 1 tablespoon grated Parmesan cheese
- 1 tomato, sliced
- 1 cup of fresh spinach, torn
- 1 sliced red onion
- 1 fresh green chili, chopped
- 8 ounces Mozzarella cheese

How to make it

1. Preheat the oven to 425º F.
2. In a small bowl combine butter, extra virgin olive oil, garlic, sauce, basil leaves, oregano, and Parmesan cheese. Spread mixture evenly on pizza dough.
3. Arrange tomato, spinach, onion, and chili on pizza. Top with Mozzarella cheese.
4. Bake in an oven or on the grill for approximately 10 minutes until crust has turned a light golden brown.

Three Cheese Pizza

Serves 8
Prep time 10 minutes
Cook time 15 minutes
Total time 25 minutes

Ingredients

- 1 pizza dough
- 8 ounces Ricotta cheese
- 8 ounces Mozzarella cheese sliced
- 8 ounces Parmesan cheese grated
- 3 tablespoons extra virgin olive oil

How to make it

1. Preheat the oven to 475º F.
2. Drizzle olive oil onto a pizza pan.
3. Place pizza dough onto the pan. Top with olive oil on the pizza dough.

4. Using the back of a tablespoon, spread the Ricotta cheese over the crust, leaving an edge to the dough for the crust. Then top with Mozzarella slices and with Parmesan cheese.

5. Place into the preheated oven and bake for 13 to 15 minutes, until the pizza crust is golden brown and the cheese has all melted.

Chicken And Feta Cheese Pizza

Serves   8
Prep time 10 minutes
Cook time 10 minutes
Total time 20 minutes

Ingredients

- 1 pizza dough
- 2 ounce butter, melted
- 2 tablespoons extra virgin olive oil
- 6 tablespoons garlic, chopped
- 4 tablespoons Passata sauce
- 2 teaspoons dried basil
- 2 teaspoons dried oregano
- 3 tablespoons shredded Parmesan cheese
- ½ cup Feta cheese
- 1 cup ready-made cheese sauce
- 9 ounces chicken breast meat, chopped and cooked
- 1 medium tomato, sliced

How to make it

1. Preheat the oven to 425º F.

2. In a small bowl, mix together the butter, extra virgin olive oil, garlic, Passata sauce, basil, oregano, Parmesan cheese, and cheese sauce.

3. Arrange the chicken on top of the pizza dough. Pour the cheese mixture evenly over the chicken. Top with tomato and Feta cheese.

4. Bake for 12 to 15 minutes in the preheated oven, until toppings are toasted.

Chef's Notes

You can use Alfredo sauce and Mozzarella cheese on top also instead of Feta and Passata sauce. Very tasty, trust me!

Chorizo And Mushrooms Pizza

Try using Pesto sauce instead of Italian Passata sauce. If you prefer, you can add the broccoli for topping. An easy supper for one!

Remember, mushrooms are very absorbent! You should take a paper towel and brush the dirt off the mushroom.

Serves 4
Prep time 10 minutes
Cook time 15 minutes
Total time 25 minutes

Ingredients
- 1 pizza dough
- 3 large portobella mushrooms cap
- 4 tablespoons Passata sauce
- 8 oz Mozzarella cheese, grated
- 10 black olives, pitted and chopped
- 8 slices chorizo, chopped
- 3 clove garlic, chopped

How to make it

1. Preheat the oven to 425º F.

2. Place mushrooms on a baking tray, and bake for 5 minutes in the preheated oven. Remove from the oven, and spread Passata sauce in the cup of the cap. Top with Mozzarella cheese, black olives, chorizo, and garlic.

3. Bake for an additional 20 minutes, or until cheese is melted and golden.

Pecorino And Mushrooms Pizza

Serves   8
Prep time 5 minutes
Cook time 25 minutes
Total time 30 minutes

Ingredients

- 1 pound pizza dough
- 1/2 pound fresh Mozzarella cheese
- 1/4 cup diced Pecorino al Tartufo cheese
- 1 cup fresh baby spinach leaves
- 4 oyster mushrooms cut in strips
- 1/2 small red onion
- 5 small grilled artichokes
- 2 tablespoons extra virgin olive oil
- 1 tablespoon dried oregano
- Sea salt and ground black pepper to taste

How to make it

1. Preheat the oven to 475º F.
2. Saute mushrooms and onion in olive oil for 4 - 5 minutes on high heat.
3. Remove from heat and add spinach, salt, pepper and mix well then let cool. The heat from the onion and mushroom will cook the baby spinach leaves.
4. Place pizza dough, drizzle with extra virgin olive oil, top with oregano and Mozzarella cheese.
5. Add sauteed mushrooms, onions and spinach leaves, then add artichokes cut in quarters and sprinkle with the diced Pecorino al Tartufo cheese.
6. Bake pizza for 10 minutes, or until crust is golden brown and cheese is bubbling.

Pepperoni And Gouda Cheese Pizza

Serves   8
Prep time 5 minutes
Cook time 10 minutes
Total time 15 minutes

　　　Ingredients

- 1 pizza dough
- 1/3 cup Passata (or Marinara or any tomato sauce)
- 2 cups Gouda cheese, grated
- 6 large slices un-cured pepperoni
- 1/4 cup Parmesan cheese, finely grated
- 1 teaspoon Italian seasoning

How to make it

1. Preheat the oven to 475º F.
2. Place pizza dough circle on a sheet of parchment paper.
3. Spread the tomato sauce on top of the dough.
4. Sprinkle the grated Gouda cheese over the sauce, again leaving a clean edge.
5. Place your pepperoni slices on top of the cheese. Sprinkle with the remaining Gouda, the finely grated Parmesan cheese and the Italian seasoning.
6. Carefully slide the pizza and the parchment paper onto the preheated pizza stone. Bake until the cheese is melted and bubbly, for 6 - 8 minutes.

Chicken and barbecue pizza

You can choose the sauce your personal taste preference.

Serves 8
Prep time 10 minutes
Cook time 30 minutes
Total time 40 minutes

Ingredients

- 1 pizza dough
- 1 cup barbecue sauce
- 2 ½ cups shredded chicken
- 8 oz Mozzarella cheese, grated
- 1/2 red onion (cut into slices)
- 4 oz Parmesan cheese, grated
- 4 tablespoons fresh parsley, chopped, optional

How to make it

1. Preheat the oven to 475º F.
2. Place pizza dough on a cornmeal or parchment paper covered pizza peel, or flat baking sheet if using a pizza stone.
3. Spread the BBQ sauce on top of the dough.
4. Place shredded chicken on top of sauce. Cover chicken with a layer of Mozzarella cheese.
5. Add onion slices on top of the cheese.
6. Sprinkle with grated Parmesan cheese.

7. Place in preheated oven and cook for 8 - 10 minutes, until golden brown and the cheese is bubbling.

8. Sprinkle fresh parsley over the pizza before serving...enjoy!

Hawaiian Pizza

Serves 8
Prep time 10 minutes
Cook time 45 minutes
Total time 55 minutes

Ingredients

- 1 ½ pounds pizza dough
- 2 tablespoons extra virgin olive oil
- ½ cup Passata sauce (or any tomato sauce)
- 2 cups Mozzarella cheese, grated
- 1 ounce thin sliced ham
- 2 ounces pineapple tidbits, drained
- ¼ cup Parmesan cheese, grated
- 12" cast iron skillet
- Fresh parsley to garnish

How to make it

1. Preheat the oven to 475º F.

2. Swirl 2 tablespoons of extra virgin olive oil around the bottom and sides of a 12-inch cast iron skillet.

3. Press pizza dough into the skillet, pressing gently up the sides. Cover and set aside in a warm place to double in size, 30 to 40 minutes. Gently press dough up the sides if it has fallen down.

4. Spread the Passata sauce on top of the dough.

5. Sprinkle Mozzarella cheese over sauce. Add slices of ham and sprinkle with pineapple tidbits.

6. Add grated Parmesan cheese over the top of pizza and place in the oven.

7. Bake for 25 to 30 minutes, until golden brown and the cheese, is melted and bubbly.

Cheeseburger Pizza

Serves 6
Prep time 10 minutes
Cook time 45 minutes
Total time 55 minutes

Ingredients

- 1 pizza dough
- ½ cup barbecue sauce
- 1 pound grass-fed 80% ground beef
- 1 cup Cheddar cheese, shredded
- 5-6 slices uncured bacon
- 1 onion, rings
- ½ head lettuce, shredded
- 1 medium tomato, diced

How to make it

1. Preheat the oven to 425º F.
2. Cook and drain bacon slices. Chop bacon, set aside.
3. Brown the ground beef in a large skillet. Drain off excess fat.
4. Cover top of dough with barbecue sauce, leaving a clean edge.
5. Sprinkle ground beef over sauce.
6. Add the shredded cheese over the top of sauce and chopped bacon.
7. Add the onion rings.

8. Slide onto the preheated baking stone and bake for 20 - 25 minutes, or until golden brown and the cheese is melted and bubbly.

9. Serve shredded lettuce and tomatoes.

Shrimp Garlic-Lemon Pizza

Serves 8
Prep time 10 minutes
Cook time 40 minutes
Total time 50 minutes

Ingredients

- 1 pound pizza dough
- 2 tablespoons extra virgin olive oil
- 2 tablespoons unsalted butter
- ¼ cup white wine
- 1 lemon zest and juice
- 1 pounds 16 count fresh shrimp peeled, deveined, and rinsed
- 1 cup Mozzarella cheese, shredded
- ¼ cup Parmesan cheese, grated
- 3 cloves garlic, minced
- ¾ teaspoon Italian seasoning

How to make it

1. Place a baking stone in oven and preheat to 425º F for 30-50 minutes.

2. In a large skillet, melt butter and olive oil over medium-low heat. Add the garlic and lemon zest, cook for 1 minute.
3. Add the white wine and lemon juice, simmer for 2 minutes.
4. Add shrimp and cook only until pink. Remove from pan and set aside.
5. Roll out pizza dough.
6. Brush dough with garlic-lemon sauce.
7. Top with shrimp, Mozzarella cheese, Parmesan cheese, and sprinkle with Italian seasoning.
8. Slide pizza onto preheated baking stone and bake for 8 to 10 minutes, until cheese is bubbly.
9. Serve with red hot pepper flakes.

Shrimp Pesto Pizza

Serves   6
Prep time 15 minutes
Cook time 15 minutes
Total time 30 minutes

   Ingredients

- 1 pound pizza dough
- 1/3 cup Pesto sauce
- ½ pound raw shrimp, cleaned and deveined
- ½ cup Mozzarella cheese, shredded
- ½ cup Feta cheese, crumbled
- 2 tablespoons white wine
- ½ tablespoon lemon juice
- 2 medium sun-dried tomatoes, sliced
- Italian seasoning to taste

How to make it

1. Place a baking stone in oven and preheat to 425º F for 30-50 minutes.

2. In a large bowl, toss shrimp with 2 tablespoons of Pesto sauce. Add the white wine and lemon juice, simmer for 2 minutes.

3. Roll out pizza dough.

4. Spread ¼ cup of Pesto sauce over the top of the pizza dough. Then place the shrimp on top of the sauce.

5. Sprinkle with Mozzarella cheese, Feta cheese, and add the tomato slices. Top with Italian seasoning.

6. Bake for 8 to 10 minutes, until cheese, is bubbly.

Green Pizza

Serves 8
Prep time 15 minutes
Cook time 5 minutes
Total time 20 minutes

Ingredients

- 1 pizza dough
- ½ cup basil Pesto sauce
- 7 cups fresh arugula
- ½ cup Parmesan cheese, grated
- 1 tablespoon extra virgin olive oil
- sea salt and ground black pepper to taste

How to make it

1. Place a baking stone in oven and preheat to 475º F for 30-50 minutes before you are ready to cook your pizza.
2. Place pizza dough on a sheet of parchment paper.
3. Top of pizza dough with extra virgin olive oil.
4. Slide parchment paper and pizza dough onto the hot baking stone.

5. Bake for 3 minutes until lightly golden brown.
6. After that, spread with basil pesto sauce.
7. Top with arugula leaves, drizzle with some olive oil, sea salt, and pepper.
8. Serve with grated Parmesan cheese.

Four Seasons Pizza

Serves   8
Prep time 5 minutes
Cook time 20 minutes
Total time 25 minutes

Ingredients

- 1 pizza dough
- 2 tablespoons extra virgin olive oil
- 1 cup Passata sauce
- 3 oz chestnut mushrooms, sliced
- ½ cup Mozzarella cheese, cut into small cubes
- ½ cup olives, quartered
- 3 oz sliced ham, cut into strips
- 6 artichokes hearts, drained and quartered
- Sea salt and fresh ground black pepper

How to make it

1. Heat the oil in a large frying pan over a high heat, and fry the mushrooms for 5 minutes stirring frequently. Season with sea salt, leave to cool and set aside.
2. Preheat the oven to 475º F.
3. Gently lift the pizza dough onto the oiled baking trays.
4. Spread the Passata sauce evenly over the pizza and season with sea salt and black pepper. Scatter the Mozzarella cheese on top.

5. Top with olives, ham, artichokes and then with mushrooms.
6. Cook in the middle of the oven for 15 minutes until golden brown.

Anchovies And Capers Pizza

A great authentic Italian recipe!
Serves 8
Prep time 5 minutes
Cook time 15 minutes
Total time 20 minutes

Ingredients

- 1 pizza dough
- 1 pound tomatoes, chopped
- 1 tablespoon extra-virgin olive oil
- 15 anchovy fillets, drained
- ½ cup green olives, drained and halved
- 1 tablespoon capers, drained
- 2 garlic cloves, thinly sliced
- 3 teaspoons dried oregano

How to make it

1. Preheat the oven to 475º F.
2. Place the pizza dough and spread chopped tomatoes over the top.

3. Scatter over the anchovies, olives, capers, garlic, and dried oregano. Drizzle with the remaining olive oil.
4. Bake for 15–20 minutes or until golden brown.

Zucchini And Chili Pizza

Serves 8
Prep time 5 minutes
Cook time 25 minutes
Total time 30 minutes

Ingredients

- 1 pizza dough
- 4 tablespoons extra virgin olive oil
- 1 zucchini, cut into cubes
- 1 ½ cup tomatoes, chopped
- ½ teaspoon chili flakes, dried
- 3 garlic cloves, chopped
- 12 anchovy fillets, drained
- 1 teaspoon fresh oregano, dried
- Sea salt

How to make it

1. Preheat the oven to 475º F.

2. Heat 3 tablespoons of the olive oil in a medium pan over medium heat. Add the zucchini, then season with salt and fry for 10 to 12 minutes, stirring occasionally. Leave to cool.

3. Put the tomatoes in a blender with the remaining 1 tablespoon of the olive oil, sea salt, and the chili flakes.

4. Spread the tomato puree evenly over the pizza dough, leaving a border clear. Scatter over the garlic and cooled zucchini and lay the anchovies on top.

5. Bake for 10–12 minutes or until golden brown.
6. Remove from the oven, sprinkle over the oregano and bake for 1 further minute.

Pizza Fiorentina

The classic Italian recipe of Florence cuisine (Italy).

Serves 8
Prep time 5 minutes
Cook time 25 minutes
Total time 30 minutes

Ingredients

- 1 pizza dough
- 2 tablespoons extra virgin olive oil
- 1 ½ cup baby spinach leaves
- 1 cup Mozzarella cheese, cut into small cubes
- 2 fresh eggs
- ¼ cup Parmesan cheese, freshly-grated
- Sea salt to taste

How to make it

1. Preheat the oven to 425º F.
2. Squeeze the spinach for the topping between your hands to remove any excess water. Set aside.
3. Place pizza dough on the oiled baking tray.
4. Brush the top of the pizza with 2 tablespoons of oil, then scatter with the Mozzarella cheese and spinach leaves, leaving an empty 2" circle in the center.

5. Bake in the oven for 8 to 10 minutes.

6. Remove the tray from the oven and crack an egg into the center of the pizza.

7. Continue baking for a further 8 minutes, adding the Parmesan cheese over the top 2 minutes before the end of the cooking time.

8. Serve and enjoy hot.

Part 2

Introduction

Who doesn't love pizza? Pizza is the ultimate food. It is quick to make an easy clean-up meal, and always a hit for any occasion be it family, social feasts, parties, and night out with a friend. Pizza is so yummy that it is the favorite in every group, be it kids or adults. Its versatility makes this tasty comfort food perfect to serve as a full meal, snack or dessert.

This cookbook catalogs two comprehensive collections of delicious gourmet vegetarian and meaty pizza recipes respectively that can be prepared at home with common pantry ingredients. These pizzas are incredibly delicious that you will stop buying ready make pizzas from the market and will lose your desire to order a takeout. From vegan to gluten-free pizza, vegetarian to meaty pizza, bake to grilled pizza, tortilla to whole-wheat base, in addition to delicious options, you will find something for yourself.

Of course, the key to a delicious pizza is pizza dough. For your convenience, 16-ounce pizza dough is directly added to each recipe. Follow the direction of the recipe below to whip your batch of pizza dough.

Healthy Vegetarian Pizzas

Stuffed Waffle Pizza

Simple to make, gluten free pepperoni waffle pizza is amazingly delicious and is a perfect a quick fix breakfast and snack.

Yield: About 1 waffle
Total Time: 25 minutes
    INGREDIENTS
1 gluten free waffle, frozen
3 tablespoons pizza sauce

6 slices of pepperoni

2 tablespoons fat-free shredded mozzarella cheese

DIRECTIONS

- Switch on broiler and preheat.
- Switch on the toaster, set to medium heat setting, place a waffle and heat for 2 minutes or until thoroughly warm and crisp.
- Spread pizza sauce onto warm waffle, then top with pepperoni slices and spread evenly with cheese.
- Place waffle in a baking tray and place in broiler for 2-3 minutes or until cheese melts and the top is a nice golden brown.

NUTRITIONAL INFORMATION PER SERVING:

250 Cal, 4g total fat (2 g sat. fat), 0 mg chol., 415 mg sodium, 15g carb., 3 g fiber, 6 g protein.

Two-Tomato Pizza

This flavor-packed pizza is a vibrant combination of fresh plum tomatoes. It is low fat and turns out delicious with just five ingredients.

Yield: About 1 pizza

Total Time: 40 minutes

INGREDIENTS

1 medium fresh yellow tomato

2 medium fresh red tomatoes

2 tablespoons olive oil

½ teaspoon salt

12 ounces / 340g frozen pizza dough, thawed

DIRECTIONS

- Switch on the baking oven, set the temperature at 475 degrees F and let it preheat.
- In the meantime, grease a baking tray with oil generously and set aside until when needed.
- Fill a medium saucepan half full with water, place it over medium-high flame and bring to boil.
- Blanch tomato. For this, make a shallow mark like X on the bottom of the tomato and submerge into boiling water. Cook for 30 seconds and then using slotted spoon, transfer to an ice water bath and leave for 30 seconds. Then using a sharp knife, peel away the skin from the tomato.
- Blanch red tomatoes in the same manner and then peel away the skin.
- Remove seeds from tomatoes and puree in a blender separately.

- Place dough on a baking tray and shape it into a 9 by 13-inch crust. Even spread yellow tomatoes mixture over 1/3 length of pizza crust and then spread red tomato mixture over the remaining crust.
- Drizzle with oil, sprinkle with salt and then place pan into the oven.
- Bake pizza for 20-25 minutes or until crust is nicely golden brown and top is brown.
- Remove baked pizza from oven, let it cool for 5 minutes and then slice to serve.

NUTRITIONAL INFORMATION PER SERVING:

156 Cal, 6.6 g total fat, 0 mg chol., 120 mg sodium, 16 g carb., 1 g fiber, 8 g protein.

Basil Pesto & Tomato Pizza

Spend weekend night by making this classic Italian tomato pizza that pairs well with bold flavor of basil pesto.

Yield: About 1 pizza
Total Time: 30 minutes

INGREDIENTS

16 ounces / 450g frozen pizza dough, thawed

3 medium tomatoes

6 ounces / 170g fat-free shredded mozzarella cheese

3 tablespoons basil pesto

¾ teaspoon salt

½ teaspoon ground black pepper

DIRECTIONS

- Switch on the baking oven, set the temperature at 500 degrees F and let it preheat.
- In the meantime, grease a 14-inch pizza pan with oil generously and set aside until require.
- Cut each tomato into 1/8-inch slices.
- Transfer dough onto a clean working space, dusted with flour lightly. Pat dough and using rolling pin shape dough into 12 inch diameter round crust. Roll crust, then unroll over prepared pizza pan and gently press it to the edges.
- Spread pesto evenly over crust and leave 1 inch edge. Sprinkle with cheese and then evenly arrange tomato slices.
- Season with salt and black pepper and then place pan into the oven.

- Bake pizza for 10-12 minutes or until crust is nicely golden brown and top is brown.
- Remove baked pizza from oven, let cool for 5 minutes and then slice to serve.

NUTRITIONAL INFORMATION PER SERVING:
228 Cal, 10.5 g total fat, 12 mg chol., 207 mg sodium, 22 g carb., 2 g fiber, 12 g protein.

Eggplant & Parmesan Cheese

This healthy pizza is packed with the flavors of crunchy eggplant slices and parmesan cheese. Serve this pizza with a green salad and have it even for breakfast.

Yield: About 1 pizza
Total Time: 50 minutes
   INGREDIENTS
16 ounces / 450g frozen pizza dough, thawed
16 ounces / 450g eggplants
1 egg white

8 fluid ounces / 236ml pasta sauce

8 ounces / 180g fat-free shredded mozzarella cheese

2 ounces / 45g cup grated parmesan cheese

2 ounces / 60g breadcrumbs, seasoned

DIRECTIONS

- Switch on the baking oven, set the temperature at 375 degrees F and let it preheat.
- In the meantime, grease a 14" inch pizza pan and set aside until necessary.
- Peel eggplants and cut into even slices. Dip each slice into egg white, cover with crumbs and then place onto the prepared baking tray.
- Place the baking tray into an oven and bake for 10 minutes until both sides nicely turn brown.
- Remove eggplant slices from oven, switch temperature of the oven to 400 degrees F and let heat.
- Transfer dough onto a clean working space, dusted with flour. Pat dough and using rolling pin shape dough into12 inch diameter round crust. Roll crust, then unroll the prepared pizza pan over and gently press it to the edges.
- Spread pizza sauce over crust, leave about 1-inch edge. Arrange baked eggplant slices, cover with cheeses and place the pan into the oven.
- Bake pizza for 12-15 minutes or until crust and top is nicely golden brown.
- Remove baked pizza from oven, let it cool for 5 minutes and then slice to serve.

NUTRITIONAL INFORMATION PER SERVING:
285 Cal, 11 g total fat (4.4 g sat. fat), 74.5 mg chol., 745 mg sodium, 35.7 g carb., 7.5 g fiber, 19.9 g protein.

Vegan Green Pizza

This pizza is clean, meatless, dairy-free and low calorie. Creamy kale pesto, olives, broccoli, chickpeas, artichoke hearts, onion, and nuts make this vegan pizza a tasty and healthy meal.
Yield: About 1 pizza
Total Time: 30 minutes
INGREDIENTS
16 ounces / 470g fresh kale, divided
½ teaspoon salt, divided
½ teaspoon ground black pepper, divided
1 tablespoons olive oil
4 ounces sunflower seeds
2 teaspoons minced garlic

1 tablespoon lemon juice

16 ounces / 450g frozen whole-wheat pizza dough, thawed

4 ounces / 115g chickpeas, cooked

4 ounces / 115g broccoli florets

1 small white onion

10 kalamata olives

5 artichokes hearts

2 ounces / 60g pine nuts

2 ounces / 60g basil leaves

2 ounces / 60g mint leaves

DIRECTIONS

- Switch on the baking oven, set the temperature at 428 degrees F and preheat.
- In the meantime, grease a 14-inch pizza pan with oil and set aside until necessary.
- Chop kale leaves and place half of the kale in a blender, reserve remaining kale for topping.
- Into a blender, add garlic, lemon juice, sunflower seeds, ¼ teaspoon ground black pepper, remaining oil and salt, and pulse until smooth. Tip pesto into a bowl and set aside until necessary.
- Transfer the dough to a clean working space, dusted with flour. Pat dough using rolling pin which will shape dough into a 12-inch diameter round crust. Roll crust, then unroll it over prepared pizza pan and gently press it to the edges.

- Place pan into the oven for 3 minutes or until crust is nicely golden brown.
- While the crust bakes, peel an onion and cut into thin rings. Pit olives and cut each into half. Cut each artichoke heart in half.
- Remove pizza pan from oven, flip crust upside-down and then evenly spread with prepared kale pesto, leave 1-inch edge.
- Spread reserve kale leaves over crust, then arrange broccoli florets, scatter with chickpeas, top with artichoke hearts, olives, onion rings and nuts.
- Drizzle oil over crust, season with remaining black pepper and return pan to oven.
- Bake pizza for 7-10 minutes or until crust is nicely golden brown.
- Remove baked pizza from oven, let cool for 5 minutes, garnish with basil and mint leaves and then slice to serve.

NUTRITIONAL INFORMATION PER SERVING:
283 Cal, 14 g total fat (4 g sat. fat), 19 mg chol., 512 mg sodium, 33 g carb., 3g fiber, 15 g protein.

Chinese Pizza With Tofu

This pizza is a vegetarian version of Chinese chicken pizza. This Chinese pizza has tamari-ginger & garlic flavored tofu and hoisin sauce. Red pepper boast flavored, and green onions and cilantro add freshness.

Yield: About 1 pizza

Total Time: 65 minutes

INGREDIENTS

14 ounces fat-free tofu, firmed

1 tablespoon sesame oil, and more as needed

1 tablespoon gluten-free tamari

1 teaspoon minced garlic

2 teaspoons minced ginger

1 small red pepper

2 tablespoons chopped green onion

1 tablespoon chopped cilantro

1 tablespoon hoisin sauce

8 ounces / 225g frozen gluten-free pizza dough, thawed

DIRECTIONS

- In a medium sized bowl stir together sesame oil, tamari, garlic and ginger until it combines well.

- Press tofu in a tofu pressure for 15 minutes or until water is out and then cut into even slices.
- Add tofu into sesame oil mixture and toss until it becomes coated. Let's marinate for 45 minutes.
- In the meantime, chop red pepper.
- Switch on the baking oven, set the temperature at 350 degrees F and let it preheat. Grease a 9-inch pizza pan and set it aside until necessary
- Transfer dough onto a clean working space, dusted with flour. Pat dough and use a rolling pin to shape dough into a 7-inch diameter round crust. Roll crust, then unroll it over prepared pizza pan and gently press it to the edges.
- Place a non-stick wok over medium flame, add two tablespoons sesame oil and heat until hot. Add marinated tofu in a single layer and sauté for 5-7 minutes per side or until it turns golden brown on all sides. Cook remaining tofu slices in the same manner and then crumble.
- Spread hoisin sauce onto pizza crust, leave 1-inch edge, spread with tofu and sprinkle with red pepper.
- Place pizza pan into oven, switch temperature to 450 degrees F and bake for 10-12 minutes or until the crust is nicely golden brown and pepper is tender.
- Remove baked pizza from oven, let it cool for 5 minutes, garnish with cilantro and green onion and then slice to serve.

NUTRITIONAL INFORMATION PER SERVING:
264 Cal, 8 g total fat (1.2 g sat. fat), 45 mg chol., 405 mg sodium, 37.8 g carb., 3.6 g fiber, 10.4 g protein.

Barbecue Tofu Pizza

Barbecue tofu pizza is a delicious pizza that is free from meat and cheese. Moreover, it tastes exactly like the real barbecue chicken pizza.
Yield: About 1 pizza
Total Time: 35 minutes
INGREDIENTS
14 ounces fat-free tofu, firmed
½ teaspoon salt
¼ teaspoon ground black pepper
2 ounces / 38g cornstarch
2 fluid ounces / 60ml olive oil
16 ounces / 450g frozen pizza dough, thawed
8 fluid ounces / 235ml barbecue sauce
1 small red onion

13 ounces fat-free shredded mozzarella cheese

2 ounces chopped cilantro

DIRECTIONS

- Press tofu in a tofu pressure for 15 minutes or until water is out and then cut into even slices.
- In a bowl combine cornstarch, salt and black pepper and then evenly cover tofu slices.
- Place a non-stick wok over medium-high flame, add oil and heat until hot. Add covered tofu slices in a single layer to wok and cook for 10 minutes per side or until it turns golden brown on all sides.
- Cook the remaining tofu slices in the same manner and place it in a bowl. Add half of the barbecue sauce and toss until it becomes coated.
- Switch on the baking oven, set temperature at 375 degrees F and let preheat.
- In the meantime, grease a 16-inch pizza pan with oil.
- Peel onion and cut into thin rings.
- Transfer dough onto a clean working space, dusted with flour. Pat dough using a rolling pin and shape the dough into a 14 inch diameter round crust. Roll crust, then unroll over prepared pizza pan and gently press it to the edges.
- Spread remaining barbecue sauce over crust, leave 1-inch edge, top evenly with tofu mixture and arrange onion slices.

- Sprinkle cheese over crust and place pan into the oven to bake for 10-12 minutes or until crust and top is nicely golden brown.
- Remove baked pizza from oven, let cool for 5 minutes, sprinkle with ¼ teaspoon salt, garnish with cilantro and slice to serve.

NUTRITIONAL INFORMATION PER SERVING:

213.5 Cal, 5 g total fat(1.2 g sat. fat), 45 mg chol., 552.5 mg sodium, 32 g carb., 3.75 g fiber, 8.5 g protein.

Tempeh Caesar Salad Pizza

Tempeh is a great alternative for meat if you don't like tofu. This pizza is a vegan version of a traditional light chicken Caesar salad pizza. It's loaded with incredible flavors of vegetarian ranch dressing, tempeh and healthy lettuce and avocado.

Yield: About 1 pizza
Total Time: 45 minutes

INGREDIENTS

1 medium avocado
16 ounces / 450g frozen pizza dough, thawed
24 ounces chopped lettuce
3 teaspoons minced garlic
8 ounces / 220g soy mayonnaise
1 tablespoon soy butter
3 tablespoons nutritional yeast
½ teaspoon onion powder
½ teaspoon ground black pepper
¼ teaspoon ground oregano

½ teaspoon soy sauce

6 fluid ounces / 180ml soy milk

4 smoked tempeh bacon slices

DIRECTIONS

- Switch on the baking oven, set the temperature at 400 degrees F and let it preheat.
- Grease a 14-inch pizza pan with oil and set aside until needed.
- While the oven heats, prepare the ranch dressing. Place a medium saucepan, add one tablespoon oil and heat until hot. Add garlic and sauté for 1-2 minutes until it turns to golden brown and fragrant.
- Add mayonnaise, butter, yeast, onion powder, black pepper, oregano, soy sauce. Then using a whisker, stir all the sauce ingredients and then slowly whisk in milk until sauce reaches to desire thickness.
- Tip sauce in a large bowl and place in refrigerator until chill and the little bit firm.
- Now, transfer the dough to a clean working space, dusted with flour. Pat the dough by using the rolling pin, shape dough into 12-inch diameter round crust. Roll crust, then unroll over prepared pizza pan and gently press it to the edges.
- Poke crust using a fork, place pan into the oven and bake for 15-20 minutes until crust is nicely golden brown and crispy.
- While crust bakes, chop tempeh. Place a medium sized frying pan, heat one tablespoon of olive oil

- and cook tempeh slices in batches for 5-8 minutes or until evenly golden brown on all sides.
- Then transfer cooked tempeh slices onto a cutting board, then cut into strips and chop.
- Peel avocado, core and dice.
- Removed baked crust from oven and assemble the pizza. Spread prepared ranch dressing until crust is covered, leave 1-inch edge. Top with chopped lettuce, cooked tempeh bacon, avocado and drizzle with more ranch dressing.
- Remove baked pizza from oven, let cool for 5 minutes and then sprinkle lightly with crushed red pepper and slice to serve.

NUTRITIONAL INFORMATION PER SERVING:

300 Cal, 6 g total fat (1g sat. fat), 43 mg chol., 952 mg sodium, 28 g carb., 3 g fiber, 25 g protein.

Roasted Vegetables & Tempeh Pizza

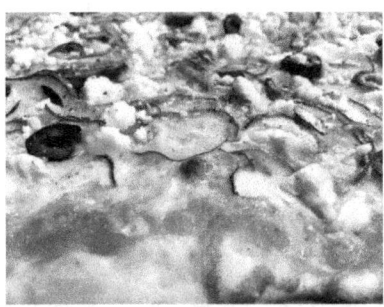

This vegan pizza is healthy, nutritious and has low calories. It is meat-free, dairy free and super delicious. It is made from simple whole-wheat dough, loaded with roasted vegetables and tempeh. You won't even miss cheese and meat in this pizza.

Yield: About 1 pizza
Total Time: 90 minutes

INGREDIENTS

16 ounces / 450g frozen whole-wheat pizza dough, thawed
2 tablespoons olive oil, and more as needed
6 fluid ounces / 170g tomato puree
¼ teaspoon Sriracha sauce
¼ teaspoon garlic powder
¼ teaspoon liquid smoke
½ cup eggplant slices
½ cup zucchini slices

5 tempeh slices

8.3 ounces / 500g cremini mushrooms

¼ teaspoon paprika powder

DIRECTIONS

- Switch on the baking oven, set the temperature at 375 degrees F and let it preheat.
- Grease a 14-inch pizza pan with oil and set aside until needed.
- In a medium sized mixing bowl, place tomato puree, add Sriracha sauce, garlic powder and liquid smoke and using a whisker stir until combine.
- Place a medium sized non-stick wok over medium-high flame, add 1 tablespoon oil and heat until hot. Add eggplant and zucchini slices in a single layer and cook for 3-5 minutes until nicely brown on all sides.
- Transfer vegetables to a separate plate and heat 1 tablespoon oil in wok. Cut each tempeh slice in half and add to batch in a single layer. Sprinkle with salt and paprika and pan-fry for 3-5 minutes or until it turns nicely golden brown.
- Transfer vegetables to a separate plate and wipe the pan clean.
- Cut mushrooms into thin slices, add to wok and roast for 5-8 minutes until mushrooms lose most of their moisture.
- Peel onion and cut into thin rings.
- Transfer dough onto a clean working space, dusted with flour. Pat dough and using a rolling pin, shape dough into 12-inch diameter round crust. Roll crust,

- then unroll over prepared pizza pan and gently press it to the edges.
- Spread prepared tomato puree mixture, leave the 1-inch edge. Top with mushrooms, zucchini and eggplant slices, and then tempeh slices.
- Place pizza pan on oven and bake pizza for 15-20 minutes until vegetables are completely cooked through, and crust is nicely golden brown.
- Remove baked pizza from oven, let cool for 5 minutes and then slice to serve.

NUTRITIONAL INFORMATION PER SERVING:

242 Cal, 8.95 g total fat (3.5 g sat. fat), 10 mg chol., 546 mg sodium, 30.9 g carb., 1.9 g fiber, 9.33 g protein.

Cauliflower Crust Pizza

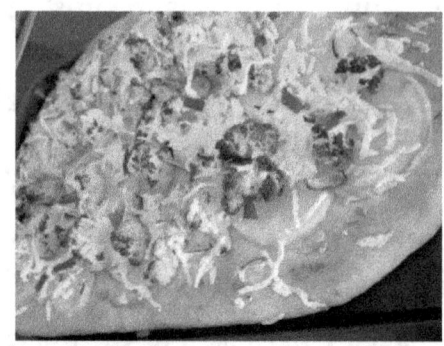

Grounded cauliflower makes a gluten-free base of this pizza. It goes best with any kind of toppings, feel free to experiment it.
Yield: About 1 pizza
Total Time: 60 minutes
    INGREDIENTS
20.3 ounces / 575g cauliflower head
16 fluid ounces / 475ml water
1 egg
3 ounces / 100g grated Parmesan cheese
¼ teaspoon salt
2 tablespoons olive oil, divided
2 fluid ounces / 60ml tomato sauce
7 ounces / 200g grated Parmesan cheese
1 small red onion
1 medium tomato
2 ounces chopped cilantro

¼ teaspoon red chili flakes

DIRECTIONS

- Switch on the baking oven, set the temperature at 400 degrees F and let it preheat.
- Cut cauliflower into floret, place it in a food processor, pour in water and pulse until smooth. Using fine sieve strain mixture, transfer the mixture into a microwaveable bowl and microwave for 5 minutes on high heat setting.
- Transfer cauliflower mixture onto a clean dish towel and squeeze out all the liquid as much as possible until completely dry.
- Place cauliflower in a bowl, add egg, salt, cheese, 1 tablespoon oil and stir until mix well.
- Line a 14-inch pizza pan with baking paper, place cauliflower mixture into the center of the pan and use wet hands to pat the mixture into a round crust as thin as possible.
- Transfer the dough to a clean working space, dusted with flour. Pat dough using a rolling pin, shape dough into a 12-inch diameter round crust. Roll crust, then unroll over prepared pizza pan and gently press it to the edges.
- Drizzle remaining oil over crust and place pan into the oven to bake for 30 minutes until crust is nicely golden brown and crisp.
- In the meantime, cut tomato into thin slices. Peel onion and cut into thin rings.

- Remove pan from oven, leave the oven on, line crust with a parchment sheet and flip upside down, then remove parchment.
- Spread tomato sauce over crust, leave 1-inch edge, spread with cheese, tomato slices and onion rings.
- Place pan into the oven to bake for 20-22 minutes or until cheese melts completely and the top is brown.
- Remove baked pizza from oven, let cool for 5 minutes, garnish with cilantro, sprinkle with red chili flakes and slice to serve.

NUTRITIONAL INFORMATION PER SERVING:

170.3 Cal, 3.2g total fat (2.8 g sat. fat), 41.8 mg chol., 2501 mg sodium, 22.3 g carb., 2.8g fiber, 16 g protein.

Corn & Black Bean Pizza

Make a full meal by serving this meatless Mexican pizza with a side salad. It is loaded with fiber, vitamins and minerals.

Yield: About 1 pizza
Total Time: 30 minutes

INGREDIENTS

1 large tomato

6 ounces / 150g cooked black beans

6 ounces / 150g fresh corn kernels

2 tablespoons cornmeal

16 ounces / 450g frozen whole-wheat pizza dough, thawed

2 fluid ounces / 80ml barbecue sauce

DIRECTIONS

- Preheat grill.
- Chop tomato and place in a bowl. Add beans and corn and stir until it mixes well.
- Take a large baking sheet and sprinkle evenly with cornmeal.
- Transfer dough onto a clean working space, dusted with flour. Pat dough using rolling pin, shape dough into 12-inch diameter round crust. Roll crust and then unroll over cornmeal so that cornmeal covers the underside of the crust.
- Transfer crust to grill, cover and cook for 4-5 minutes or until crust puffs and bottom is nicely golden brown.
- Then carefully flip crust suing spatula, then quickly spread barbecue sauce evenly over crust, leave 1-inch edge, top with tomato mixture and cover with cheese.

- Return lid and cook for another 4-5 minute until cheese melts completely and the bottom is nicely golden brown.
- Remove baked pizza from oven, let cool for 5 minutes and then slice to serve.

NUTRITIONAL INFORMATION PER SERVING:

302 Cal, 9g total fat (3 g sat. fat), 15 mg chol., 484 mg sodium, 48 g carb., 4 g fiber, 13 g protein.

Beans & Spicy Mango Pizza

Beans and spicy mango pizza is a perfect summer pizza. Trying this pizza during family pizza nights is wonderful.

Yield: About 1 pizza
Total Time: 25 minutes

INGREDIENTS

1 medium zucchini

1 medium mango

16 ounces / 45g frozen pizza dough, thawed

8 ounces / 250g hot salsa

8 ounces / 250g shredded Mexican cheese blend

2 ounces / 50g cooked black beans

1 medium green onion

2 ounces / 50g cilantro leaves

Directions

- Peel mango and zucchini and slice. Slice green onion.
- Switch on the baking oven, set the temperature at 400 degrees F and let it preheat.
- In the meantime, grease a 14-inch pizza pan with oil.
- Transfer dough onto a clean working space, dusted with flour. Pat dough using rolling pin, shape dough into a 12-inch diameter round crust. Roll crust, then unroll over prepared pizza pan and gently press it to the edges.
- Spread salsa evenly onto the crust, leave 1-inch edge. Top with Mexican cheese blend, zucchini and mango slices and beans.
- Place pan into the oven to bake for 15-20 minutes or until crust and top turns golden brown.
- Remove baked pizza from oven, let cool for 5 minutes, garnish with green onion and cilantro, and slice to serve.

NUTRITIONAL INFORMATION PER SERVING:

130 Cal, 4.8 g total fat (1.8 g sat. fat), 7.5 mg chol., 7.5 mg sodium, 14.8 g carb., 3g fiber, 6.4 g protein.

Artichoke, Broccoli And Spinach Pesto Pizza

This green, super healthy and nutritious pizza is loaded with the creamy spinach pesto with a hint of cheese, broccoli and artichoke heart and feta.

Yield: About 1 pizza
Total Time: 55 minutes

INGREDIENTS

2 ounces / 50g chopped walnuts
8 ounces / 200g spinach leaves
8 ounces / 200g basil leaves
2 teaspoons garlic
¾ teaspoon salt
¼ teaspoon ground black pepper
4 fluid ounces / 120ml olive oil
4 ounces / 100g grated Parmesan cheese
16 ounces / 450g frozen pizza dough, thawed
14 ounces / 350g artichoke hearts
18 ounces / 510g broccoli heads
16 ounces / 400g crumbled feta cheese

DIRECTIONS

- Switch on the baking oven, set the temperature at 425 degrees F and let it preheat.
- In the meantime, grease a 14-inch pizza pan with oil.
- Prepare spinach pesto. Place a small non-stick skillet pan over medium flame, add walnuts and cook for 3-5 minutes or until lightly toasted, stir often. Then remove walnuts from heat and let it cool.
- Place spinach, basil, garlic, walnuts Into a blender and pulse until minced.
- Add salt, black pepper, olive oil, cheese and pulse until it's smooth. Tip pesto into a bowl and set aside until needed,
- Cut broccoli into florets, place it in a microwaveable bowl and microwave for 3-5 minutes or until tender. Strain broccoli in a fine sieve to drain its liquid and set aside until cool.
- While broccoli cools off, transfer dough onto a clean working space, dusted with flour. Pat dough using a rolling pin, then shape dough into a 12-inch diameter round crust. Roll crust, then unroll over prepared pizza pan and gently press it to the edges.
- Spread evenly with prepared pesto, leave 1-inch edge. Sprinkle with ½ portion of feta and evenly top with broccoli. Quarter each artichoke and distribute evenly over broccoli layer.
- Sprinkle with remaining feta cheese and place pan into the oven to bake for 30-35 minutes or until

crust and top is nicely golden brown and vegetables are cooked through.
- Remove baked pizza from oven, let cool for 5 minutes and then slice to serve.

NUTRITIONAL INFORMATION PER SERVING:

283 Cal, 14 g total fat (4 g sat. fat), 19 mg chol., 512 mg sodium, 33 g carb., 3g fiber, 15 g protein.

Chocolate Pizza

One word for this pizza, heavenly! This unique chocolate pizza is an ultimate dessert and can also serve as a dessert to impress your love one or celebrate special occasions with it.

Yield: About 1 pizza

Total Time: 30 minutes

INGREDIENTS

16 ounces / 450g frozen pizza dough, thawed

2 teaspoons fat-free butter, melted

2 ounces / 60g chocolate hazelnut spread

3 ounces / 90g chocolate chips

2 tablespoons milk chocolate chips

2 tablespoons white chocolate chips

2 tablespoons chopped hazelnuts

DIRECTIONS

- Switch on the baking oven, set the temperature at 375 degrees F and let it preheat.

- In the meantime, grease a large baking tray with oil and set aside until needed.
- Transfer dough to a clean working space dusted with flour. Pat dough using rolling pin shape dough into 9-inch diameter round crust. Roll crust, then unroll over prepared baking tray using your fingers to make indentation all over the crust.
- Brush crust with butter and place baking tray in the oven to bake for 15-20 minutes until nicely golden brown.
- Remove crust from oven and immediately spread with hazelnut spread and sprinkle evenly with all the chocolate chips.
- Return pizza to oven and bake for another 1-2 minutes or until chocolate chips begin to melt.
- Remove baked pizza from oven, let cool for 5 minutes, garnish with hazelnuts and slice to serve.

NUTRITIONAL INFORMATION PER SERVING:

190 Cal, 11 g total fat (6 g sat. fat), 5 mg chol., 40 mg sodium, 21 g carb., 1 g fiber, 2 g protein.

Raspberry Brie Pizza

This Brie cheese pizza is unique and offers luxurious texture and extraordinary softness that pairs well with raspberry.

Yield: About 1 pizza
Total Time: 35 minutes

INGREDIENTS

8.5 ounces / 240g frozen wewalka bistro style pizza dough, thawed

2 tablespoons fat-free butter

5 ounces walnuts

¼ teaspoon ground cinnamon

2 tablespoons brown sugar

3 ounces brie cheese

1 tablespoon olive oil

3 ounces / 95g raspberry preserves

7 ounces / 200g fresh raspberries

1 teaspoon chopped rosemary

DIRECTIONS

- Switch on the baking oven, set the temperature at 400 degrees F and let it preheat.
- In the meantime, place a small saucepan over medium flame, add butter and heat for 2-3 minutes or until it melts. Add walnuts, cinnamon and sugar and stir to mix. Cook mixture for 4-5 minute or until sugar caramelizes. Then transfer the nut mixture to a wax paper, spread evenly and let it cool completely.
- Line a medium sized baking tray with parchment sheet and place pizza dough. Brush evenly with oil. Thinly slice brie cheese and arrange onto pizza dough and around each slice of cheese, drop a spoon of jam and then evenly arrange half of the raspberries.
- Sprinkle rosemary over pizza and place the baking tray into the oven.
- Bake pizza for 12-15 minutes until crust is nicely golden brown.
- Remove baked pizza from oven, let cool for 5 minutes, then garnish with remaining raspberries and walnuts mixture and slice to serve.

Nutritional Information Per Serving:

281 Cal, 14 g total fat (5 g sat. fat), 45 mg chol., 205 mg sodium, 23 g carb., 2 g fiber, 16 g protein.

Meat Lover Pizzas

Chinese Chicken Hoisin Pizza

In this recipe, an Asian chicken pizza is present with a tasty twist that is chicken flavored with hoisin sauce.
Yield: About 1 pizza
Total Time: 40 minutes

INGREDIENTS

16 ounces / 450g frozen pizza dough, thawed
1 large white onion
6 medium green onions
7.5 ounces / 211g shredded cooked chicken
2 teaspoons minced garlic
1 tablespoon minced ginger
3 tablespoons hoisin sauce & more as needed
1 teaspoon Sambal Oelek
6.5 ounces / 181g fat-free shredded mozzarella cheese

2 ounces / 60.3g chopped cilantro

DIRECTIONS

- Switch on the baking oven, set the temperature at 500 degrees F and let it preheat.
- In the meantime, grease a 14-inch pizza pan with oil and set aside until needed.
- Peel green onions, cut diagonally into thin slice and place in a medium-sized bowl. Add shredded chicken in a bowl, add garlic, ginger, hoisin sauce, Sambal oelek and toss to coat well.
- Transfer dough onto a clean working space, dusted with flour. Pat dough using rolling pin, shape dough into 12-inch diameter round crust. Roll crust, then unroll over prepared pizza pan and gently press it to the edges.
- Spread ¼ cup hoisin sauce over crust, leave 1-inch edge.
- Peel white onion, slice and spread over crust and then top with chicken mixture. Cover with cheese and place pan into the oven.
- Bake pizza for 10-12 minutes or until crust is turns golden brown and top is brown.
- Cut remaining green onions diagonally into thin slices.
- Remove baked pizza from oven, let cool for 5 minutes, sprinkle with cilantro and then slice to serve.

NUTRITIONAL INFORMATION PER SERVING:

316 Cal, 14.5g total fat (6.8 g sat. fat), 80 mg chol., 786 mg sodium, 19.4 g carb., 2.2 g fiber, 26.6 g protein.

Chicken Garlic Pizza

Impress family by baking this chicken garlic pizza that taste exactly like the restaurant one and turns out in less than 30 minutes.

Yield: About 1 pizza
Total Time: 25 minutes

INGREDIENTS

1 big tomato

6 ounces / 170g chicken breast, grilled

16 ounces / 450g frozen pizza dough, thawed

6 ounces / 170g ranch dressing

1 tablespoon minced garlic

12 ounces / 340g fat-free shredded mozzarella cheese

2 ounces / 60g grated non-fat cheddar cheese

1.5 ounces / 45g grated Parmesan cheese

2 ounces / 15g chopped green onions

DIRECTIONS

- Switch on the baking oven, set temperature at 425 degrees F and let it preheat.

- In the meantime, grease a 14-inch pizza pan with oil.
- Transfer dough onto a clean working space, dusted with flour. Pat dough using rolling pin shape dough into 12-inch diameter round crust. Roll crust, then unroll over prepared pizza pan and gently press it to the edges.
- In a medium bowl stir together ranch dressing and garlic until mix well and then spread dressing evenly on the crust, leave 1-inch edge.
- In another medium sized bowl combine all the cheeses and then evenly spread half of the mixture over sauce layer on the crust.
- Slice chicken and arrange on cheese layer. Dice tomato and scatter over chicken layer and top with green onion. Cover with remaining cheeses mixture and place pan into the oven.
- Bake pizza for 12-15 minutes until the cheese melts and the crust and top are nicely golden brown.
- Remove baked pizza from oven, let it cool for 5 minutes and then slice to serve.

NUTRITIONAL INFORMATION PER SERVING:
320 Cal, 15 g total fat (6 g sat. fat), 35 mg chol., 600 mg sodium, 30 g carb., 1 g fiber, 18 g protein.

Chicken, Bacon & Strawberry Pizza

This unique pizza accompanies flavorful chicken and smoked bacon in addition to the fresh strawberry and plenty of cheese.

Yield: About 1 pizza
Total Time: 40 minutes
    INGREDIENTS
4 ounces / 120g strawberry Jam
2 fluid ounces / 60ml apple cider vinegar
1 teaspoon Sriracha Sauce
16 ounces / 45g frozen pizza dough, thawed
6 ounces / 170g chicken breast, cooked
4 ounces / 110g smoked bacon
1 medium sweet onion
12 ounces / 340g Italian cheese blend
2 ounces / 50g cilantro

2 ounces / 50g Fresh strawberries

DIRECTIONS

- Switch on the baking oven, set temperature at 450 degrees F and let it preheat.
- In the meantime, grease a 14-inch pizza pan with oil.
- Place a small saucepan over medium flame, pour vinegar and bring to boil. Then reduce heat and simmer vinegar for 4-5 minutes or until it reduces to half and consistency is thick and syrupy.
- Remove saucepan from the flame, add jam and Sriracha, stir until combine and set aside until cool.
- While mixture cools off, transfer the dough onto a clean working space, dusted with flour. Pat dough using rolling pin, shape dough into a 12-inch diameter round crust. Roll crust, then unroll over prepared pizza pan and gently press it to the edges.
- Dice chicken, place in a bowl, add 2 tablespoons of prepared raspberry mixture and toss to coat completely.
- Onto pizza crust, spread remaining cooked raspberry mixture, leave the 1-inch edge. Top evenly with chicken mixture and then cover with ¾ portion of cheese.
- Cut bacon into bite size pieces. Peel and thinly slice onion.
- Arrange bacon over cheese layer, followed by onion slices and then sprinkle with remaining cheese.

- Place pan in the oven to bake for 10-12 minutes or until crust and top is nicely golden brown and cheese bubbles.
- Remove baked pizza from oven, let cool for 5 minutes.
- Dice strawberries and scatter over pizza, sprinkle with cilantro and then slice to serve.

NUTRITIONAL INFORMATION PER SERVING:

270 Cal, 7 g total fat (3 g sat. fat), 90 mg chol., 250 mg sodium, 28 g carb., 3 g fiber, 19 g protein.

Meatball Pizza

Meatball pizza is a quick fix meal. Always store an extra dough and frozen meatballs and make this filling pizza any time of the day.

Yield: About 1 pizza

Total Time: 30 minutes

INGREDIENTS

16 ounces / 450g frozen pizza dough, thawed

8 ounces / 235g pizza sauce

1 teaspoon garlic powder

1 teaspoon Italian seasoning

1 small red onion

12 frozen meatballs, thawed

2 ounces / 60g grated Parmesan cheese

8 ounces / 240g fat-free shredded mozzarella cheese

DIRECTIONS

- Switch on the baking oven, set the temperature at 350 degrees F and let it preheat.
- In the meantime, grease a 14-inch pizza pan with oil.

- Transfer dough onto a clean working space, dusted with flour. Pat dough using rolling pin, shape the dough into a 12-inch diameter round crust. Roll crust, then unroll over prepared pizza pan and gently press it to the edges.
- Spread pizza sauce evenly on the crust, leave 1-inch edge, and sprinkle with Italian seasoning, garlic and parmesan cheese.
- Peel onion, cut in half, slice and scatter over crust. Arrange meatballs and cover with mozzarella cheese
- Sprinkle cheese over crust and place pan into the oven to bake for 10-12 minutes or until crust and top is nicely golden brown.
- Remove baked pizza from oven, let cool for 5 minutes and then slice to serve.

NUTRITIONAL INFORMATION PER SERVING:

280 Cal, 10 g total fat (5 g sat. fat), 25 mg chol., 710 mg sodium, 33 g carb., 1 g fiber, 15 g protein.

Pizza Cubano

All the flavors of a cubano sandwich are present in the pizza form. Flavor full mustard paste, tender chicken, crispy ham, tangy pickles and off course cheese, all in one pizza.

Yield: About 1 pizza
Total Time: 30 minutes

INGREDIENTS

1 small red onion

1 dill pickle

16 ounces / 450g frozen pizza dough, thawed

2 tablespoons yellow mustard

3 ounces / 85g chicken breast, cooked

2 ounces / 60g baked ham

4 ounces / 120g parsley

3 ounces / 85g grated Gruyere cheese

DIRECTIONS

- Switch on the baking oven, set the temperature at 375 degrees F and let it preheat.

- In the meantime, grease a 14-inch pizza pan with oil.
- Peel onion and chop. Chop pickle, shred chicken and thinly slice ham.
- Now, prepare the crust. Transfer dough onto a clean working space, dusted with flour. Pat dough using a rolling pin, shape dough into a 12-inch diameter round crust. Roll crust, then unroll over prepared pizza pan and gently press it to the edges.
- Spread mustard paste over crust, leave the 1-inch edge, sprinkle with pickle and then onion. Arrange with shredded chicken and ham. Scatter with parsley and cover with cheese.
- Place pan in the oven to bake for 12-15 minutes or until crust and top is nicely golden brown.
- Remove baked pizza from oven, let cool for 5 minutes and then slice to serve.

NUTRITIONAL INFORMATION PER SERVING:

260 Cal, 4.8 g total fat (1.7 g sat. fat), 48 mg chol., 560 mg sodium, 38 g carb., 6.4 g fiber, 22 g protein.

Pepperoni & Cheese Tortilla Pizza

In absence of a pizza crust, feel free to use a tortilla as a pizza base. Tortilla pizzas are much healthier and faster than the take-out ones.

Yield: About 1 pizza
Total Time: 25 minutes

INGREDIENTS

1 large floured tortilla
4 ounces / 120g pizza sauce
2 ounces / 120g shredded fat-free cheddar cheese
6 pepperoni pieces

DIRECTIONS

- Switch on the baking oven, set the temperature at 375 degrees F and let it preheat.
- Grease a cookie sheet with oil and place tortilla bread. Spread half of the pizza sauce evenly over bread and then sprinkle with cheese.
- Arrange pepperoni over cheese layer and place sheet in oven to bake for 5-8 minutes or until

cheese melts completely and the edges begin to crusty.
- Remove baked pizza from oven, let cool for 5 minutes and then slice to serve.

NUTRITIONAL INFORMATION PER SERVING:

247 Cal, 8.5 g total fat (2.9 g sat. fat), 16 mg chol., 611 mg sodium, 30.8 g carb., 5 g fiber, 12 g protein.

Avocado & Salmon Tortilla Pizza

This tortilla pizza is a light healthy pizza that is perfect for brunch or snack.

Yield: About 1 pizza

Total Time: 30 minutes

INGREDIENTS

1 floured tortilla

4 tablespoons fat-free cream cheese

½ tablespoon dried basil

1 teaspoon minced garlic

1 tablespoon olive oil

1 small red onion

3.5 ounces / 100g fat-free shredded mozzarella cheese

3.5 ounces / 100g smoked salmon

1 small avocado

¼ teaspoon lemon pepper

DIRECTIONS

- Switch on the baking oven, set the temperature at 400 degrees F and let it preheat.

- In a bowl, place cream cheese and using electric mixer combine with garlic and dill until mix well.
- Grease a cookie sheet with oil and place tortilla bread.
- Brush crust with oil, then spread with cream cheese mixture.
- Peel onion, cut into rings and scatter over tortilla and then cover with cheese.
- Place pan into the oven to bake for 10-12 minutes or until the cheese melts completely and the crust and top are nicely golden brown.
- Remove baked pizza from oven and let cool for 5 minutes, do not switch off oven.
- In the meantime, slice salmon. Peel the avocado and slice thinly.
- Arrange salmon slices on the pizza, then top it with avocado and sprinkle lemon pepper.
- Return pizza to oven and bake for 2-3 minutes until warm through.
- Remove pizza and slice to serve.

NUTRITIONAL INFORMATION PER SERVING:

236 Cal, 12 g total fat (1.9 g sat. fat), 45 mg chol., 519 mg sodium, 27 g carb., 4.5 g fiber, 18.8 g protein.

Shrimp & Basil Pesto Pizza

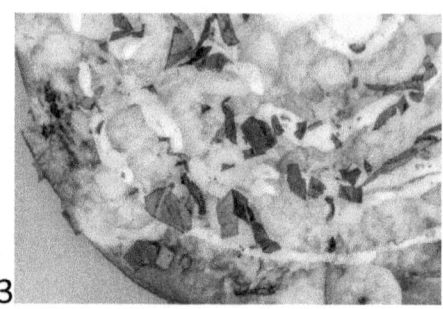

A tasty combination of creamy pesto pizza, shrimps and garden vegetables make a wonderful sea-food pizza.
Yield: About 1 pizza
Total Time: 25 minutes

INGREDIENTS

1 small red onion

2 small fresh tomatoes

3 ounces / 85g shrimps, grilled

4 ounces / 120g grated Parmesan cheese

4 ounces / 110g frozen pizza dough, thawed

2 tablespoons olive oil

½ teaspoon salt

¼ teaspoon ground black pepper

2 tablespoons basil pesto

DIRECTIONS

- Peel onion and cut into thin rings. Slice tomatoes.
- Set up the grill, heat grilling rack over medium-high flame and grease the grilling rack with oil generously.
- In the meantime, transfer the dough onto a clean working space dusted with flour. Pat dough using rolling pin, shape dough into a 10-inch diameter round crust. Brush one side of crust with olive oil and then season with salt and black pepper.
- Gently place crust on the grilling rack, oiled side down and then brush the other side with oil. Cook crust for 2-3 minutes or until underside crust is lightly charred, and then flip crust. Cook for another 1-2 minutes and then slide crust to the cool side of grilling rack.
- Immediately spread pesto over crust, leave 1-inch edge, scatter with shrimps and then with tomato and onion slices and cover with cheese. Cover grill and cook pizza for 3-5 minutes until vegetables are tender and cheese melts completely.
- Remove pizza from grill, let cool for 5 minutes and then slice to serve.

NUTRITIONAL INFORMATION PER SERVING:

234 Cal, 12 g total fat (3.6 g sat. fat), 31 mg chol., 521 mg sodium, 20 g carb., 2 g fiber, 14 g protein.

Chicken & Bacon-Basil Pesto Pizza

This easy dinner pizza accompanies combination chicken and bacon pesto that serve as a great meal.
Yield: About 1 pizza
Total Time: 45 minutes

   INGREDIENTS

16 ounces / 450g frozen pizza dough, thawed

17 ounces / 500g basil leaves

2 teaspoons minced garlic

8 bacon slices, uncooked

3 ounces / 90g grated Parmesan cheese

4 fluid ounces / 120ml olive oil

5 ounces / 140g fat-free shredded mozzarella cheese

6 ounces / 170g chicken breast, uncooked

¼ teaspoon ground black pepper

DIRECTIONS

- Switch on the baking oven, set the temperature at 425 degrees F and let it preheat.

- In the meantime, grease a 14-inch pizza pan with oil.
- Place a medium sized non-stick skillet pan over medium flame, heat 1 tablespoon oil and fry bacon in batches until nicely golden brown on all sides and cook through.
- Transfer cooked bacon to a cutting board, let it cool slightly and then chop half of the bacon, reserve remaining bacon for topping pizza.
- Wipe clean pan, add chicken breast and cook for 7-10 minutes until tender. Then transfer chicken breast to a cutting board using fork shred meat. Set aside until required.
- Now prepare pesto. In a blender place basil and garlic and pulse until it minces. Add cheese and pulse until it combines. Continue processing and blend in oil until it incorporates and becomes smooth. Tip mixture into a bowl add chopped cooked bacon and stir until it mixes .
- Transfer dough onto a clean working space, dusted with flour. Pat dough using rolling pin, shape dough into 12-inch diameter round crust. Roll crust, then unroll over prepared pizza pan and gently press it to the edges.
- Spread bacon-basil pesto evenly, leave 1-inch edge, then cover with cheese and scatter with cooked bacon slices and chicken.
- Sprinkle black pepper over pizza and place pan into the oven to bake for 15-20 minutes or until crust and top is nicely golden brown.

- Remove baked pizza from oven, let cool for 5 minutes and then slice to serve.

NUTRITIONAL INFORMATION PER SERVING:

271 Cal, 5.1 g total fat (2.3 g sat. fat), 65 mg chol., 560 mg sodium, 38 g carb., 6.4 g fiber, 22 g protein.

Chicken-Broccoli Garlic Bread Pizza

This recipe calls for garlic bread crust topped with chicken and broccoli, boosted with the flavors of Alfredo sauce and off course cheese.

Yield: About 1 pizza
Total Time: 70 minutes

    INGREDIENTS

8 fluid ounces / 250ml water, warm
1 ¼ teaspoons dry-active yeast
½ teaspoon sugar
11 ounces / 300g all-purpose flour
1 teaspoon garlic powder
½ teaspoon dried basil
½ teaspoon salt
2 tablespoons grated Parmesan cheese
6 ounces chicken breast
½ teaspoon salt
¼ teaspoon ground black pepper
4 ounces / 120g Alfredo Sauce

12 ounces / 350g broccoli florets

12 ounces / 350g fat-free shredded mozzarella cheese

3 tablespoons grated Parmesan cheese

DIRECTIONS

- Switch on the baking oven, set the temperature at 425 degrees F and let it preheat.
- Grease a 14-inch pizza pan with oil and set aside until required.
- Pour warm water in a small bowl, stir in yeast and sugar and set aside in a warm place for 5-10 minutes or until foamy.
- Using a stand mixer, place flour, garlic, basil, salt and cheese and combine all the ingredients at medium speed. Turn mixer to low speed and slowly mix yeast mixer until firm dough comes together. Mix 1-2 tablespoons flour if the dough is too sticky or mix 1-2 tablespoons water is dough is too dry.
- Transfer dough onto a clean working space, dusted with flour and kneaded dough for 5 minutes. Shape dough into a ball, place in a bowl, cover with a wet towel and let it stand in a warm place for 30-45 minutes until dough doubles in size.
- In the meantime, prepared chicken. Season chicken with salt and black pepper. Place a non-stick skillet pan over a medium flame, heat 1 tablespoon oil and place chicken. Cook chicken for 7-10 minutes or until tender and then transfer to a cutting board.
- Let chicken cool slightly and then make use of a fork shred.

- Transfer dough onto a clean working space, pat dough using a rolling pin, shape dough into a 12-inch diameter round crust. Roll crust, then unroll over prepared pizza pan and gently press it to the edges.
- Place pan into the oven to bake for 5 minutes or until crust is nicely golden brown. Remove pan from oven and immediately spread with Alfredo sauce, leave 1-inch edge. Scatter with chicken and then with broccoli. Sprinkle with cheese and return pan to oven.
- Bake pizza for 12-15 minutes until the top is nicely golden brown and cheese bubbles.
- Remove baked pizza from oven, let cool for 5 minutes and then slice to serve.

NUTRITIONAL INFORMATION PER SERVING:

380 Cal, 22 g total fat (8 g sat. fat), 25 mg chol., 680 mg sodium, 35 g carb., 2 g fiber, 14 g protein.

Pepperoni Pizza

Ingredients

1 cup plus 2 tablespoons water (70 ° to 80 °)
2 tablespoons grated Parmesan cheese
2 tablespoons olive oil
1-1 / 2 teaspoons Italian seasoning
1 teaspoon sugar
1 teaspoon salt
3 cups all-purpose flour
2-1 / 2 teaspoons active dry yeast
1 tablespoon cornmeal
TOPPINGS:
1 cup meatless spaghetti sauce
1 to 3 teaspoons sugar, optional

1 package (8 ounces) sliced pepperoni
2 medium tomatoes, chopped
1 / 2 cup chopped onion

4 cups shredded part-skim mozzarella cheese

1 / 2 cup grated Parmesan cheese

1-1 / 2 teaspoons Italian seasoning

Method

In the bread machine pan, place the first eight ingredients in order suggested by manufacturer. Select dough setting (5 minutes of mixing; add 1-2 tablespoons of water or flour if needed).

When cycle is completed, turn dough onto a lightly floured surface. Roll into a 14-in. circle. Sprinkle a greased 14-in. pizza pan with cornmeal. Transfer dough to prepared pan.

Combine spaghetti sauce and sugar if desired; spread over dough. Top with the pepperoni, tomatoes, onion, cheeses and Italian seasoning.

Bake at 400 ° for 30-35 minutes or until crust is lightly browned. Let stand for 10 minutes before cutting.

Sausage Pizza

Ingredients

1 loaf (1 pound) frozen bread dough, thawed

3 / 4 pound bulk hot Italian sausage

1 / 2 cup sliced onion

1 / 2 cup sliced fresh mushrooms

1 / 2 cup chopped green pepper

1 / 2 cup pizza sauce

2 cups shredded part-skim mozzarella cheese

Method

With greased fingers, pat dough onto an ungreased 12-in. pizza pan. Prick dough thoroughly with a fork. Bake at 400 ° for 10-12 minutes or until lightly browned. Meanwhile, in a large skillet, cook the sausage, onion, mushrooms and green pepper over medium heat until sausage is no longer pink; drain.Spread pizza sauce over crust.

Top with sausage mixture;

sprinkle with cheese. Bake at 400 ° for 12-15 minutes or until golden brown. Or wrap pizza and freeze for up to 2 months.

To use frozen pizza:

Unwrap and place on a pizza pan; thaw in the refrigerator. Bake at 400 ° for 18-22 minutes or until golden brown.

California-Style Pizza Dough

Makes dough for 4 (4-inch) individual pizzas or 1 (14-inch) pizza
Starter
1/3 cup rye or whole-wheat flour
1 (1/4-ounce) package active Rapid-rise yeast
1 / 4 cup warm water (100 degrees F to 110 degrees F)
1/4 teaspoon sugar
Dough
1 tablespoon whole milk

1 / 4 cup extra-virgin olive oil, plus extra for drizzling

1 / 2 cup warm water (100 degrees F to 110 degrees F)

1-3 / 4 cups unbleached all-purpose flour, plus extra for kneading

1 teaspoon salt

Method

To make the starter, put the rye flour in a large bowl. Sprinkle the yeast over the flour and add the water and sugar.

Lightly mix the ingredients together with a spoon until they form a thick dough. Cover the bowl with plastic wrap and place in a draft-free spot for 15 minutes.

Get set ...

To make the dough, combine the milk, 1/4 cup of olive oil, and warm water in a small bowl. Combine the unbleached flour and salt in a bowl and whisk to mix

California-Style Pizza Cheeses

Makes 4 (4-inch) individual pizzas or 1 (12-inch) pizza

4 ounces mozzarella

3 tablespoons whole milk

4 ounces soft or fresh goat cheese

1 / 4 cup freshly grated Parmesan cheese

1 bunch fresh basil

1 small bunch fresh chives

1 small bunch fresh arugula

1 ripe tomato

1 / 2 cup pitted black olives

1 / 4 cup extra-virgin olive oil

Freshly ground black pepper Sea salt

Method

On the largest holes of a four-sided grater, grate the mozzarella into a medium-size bowl. Add the milk, the goat cheese, and the parmesan cheese. Mix well to combine. Set aside.

Wash the basil and shake to remove excess water. Pull the basil leaves off the stems and discard the stems. Measure 1/2 to 3/4 cup of loosely packed basil leaves and lay them on a clean paper towel. Wrap the basil leaves in the towel to remove any excess moisture. Set the basil aside.

Wash the chives, shake to remove excess water, and dry by rolling in towels. Coarsely chop the chives, measure out 1/4 cup, and set aside.

Wash the arugula in a large bowl of cold water. Let the leaves float in the water for a few minutes so that any dirt still clinging to them can fall to the bottom of the bowl. Lift the arugula up out of the water and transfer to a colander to drain. Wash and refill the bowl with cold water and repeat this step at least once. Drain the arugula a final time.

Cut off and discard the arugula stems. Lay the arugula leaves on a few clean paper towels. Wrap the arugula leaves in the towels to remove any excess moisture. Coarsely chop the leaves, measure 1 cup loosely packed, and set aside.

Wash the tomato; cut off the stem circle at the top and discard. Cut the tomato into small chunks and set aside in a small bowl.

Chop the olives, add to the tomatoes, and toss well to combine. Set aside.

Get set ...

To make a big pie

Preheat the oven to 475 degrees F with a rack in the middle slot of the oven.

Pour about 1 tablespoon of the olive oil onto a 10-1 / 2 by 15-1 / 2 by 1-inch heavy aluminum or nonstick baking sheet and coat the bottom and sides evenly. Set the dough in the center of the tray, cover loosely with the plastic wrap, and let stand for 5 to 10 minutes. Using your fingers, spread the dough across the baking sheet until it is about 1/4-inch thick. Gently press the dough into the sides of the pan to form a ridge. Brush the entire surface with olive oil, including the sides and top of the ridge. Using a large spoon or your fingers, carefully spread the garlic butter but not the ridge of the dough Spread the arugula leaves evenly over the dough. Sprinkle the cheese mixture on top of the arugula. If the basil leaves are big, tear some of them in half. Lay them across the top of the arugula. Sprinkle on the chives. Top with the chopped tomato-and-olive combination. Drizzle the remainder of the oil of the pizza. Cook!
Bake for 15 to 20 minutes on the middle rack, until the pizza is browned and crispy. Remove the pizza from the oven and let it cool a few minutes. Gently slide into a pizza to loosen it, then carefully slide it onto a cutting board. Cut into slices with a sharp knife.
Serve hot.

Chicago-Style Deep Dish Pizza

Ingredients

8 ounces mushrooms, wiped clean and thinly sliced
Chicago Style Deep Dish Pizza Dough, recipe follows
1 green bell pepper, cored and cut into thin rings
2 tablespoons olive oil
1 tablespoon chopped fresh garlic
1 yellow onion, cut into thin rings

1 cup thinly sliced black olives
2 teaspoons chopped fresh basil
1 pound crumbled hot Italian sausage
1 teaspoon chopped fresh oregano
1 cup grated Parmesan
1/4 teaspoon fennel seeds
1/2 teaspoon salt
1/4 teaspoon freshly ground black pepper
1/4 teaspoon red pepper flakes

1 (28-ounce) can plum tomatoes, coarsely crushed
1 tablespoon dry red wine
1 teaspoon sugar
1 tablespoon extra-virgin olive oil
1 pound mozzarella cheese, sliced
8 ounces pepperoni, thinly sliced
Chicago-style Deep Dish Pizza Dough:
1 1/2 cups warm water (about 110 degrees F)
1 (1/4-ounce) packages active dry yeast
1 teaspoon sugar
3 1/2 cups all-purpose flour
1/2 cup semolina flour
1/2 cup vegetable oil, plus 2 teaspoons to grease bowl
1 teaspoon salt

Method

While the dough is rising, make the tomato sauce. In a medium saucepan, heat the oil over medium-high heat. Add the garlic and cook, stirring, for 30 seconds.

Add the herbs, seeds, salt, and black and red peppers, and cook, stirring, for 30 seconds. Add the tomatoes, wine and sugar, and bring to a boil. Lower the heat and simmer, stirring occasionally, until thickened, 20 to 30 minutes. Remove from the heat and let cool before using.

Preheat the oven to 475 degrees F.

Oil 2 seasoned 12-inch round deep-dish pizza with extra-virgin olive oil. Press 1 piece of dough into each pan, pressing to the edge and stretching about 1 1/2 inches up the sides. Let rest for 5 minutes.

Layer the mozzarella cheese all over the bottom of the pies. Top each with half of the pepperoni, mushrooms, bell pepper rings, onions, black olives and sausage. The top is golden and the cheese is bubbly and the crust is golden brown, about 30 minutes. Remove from the oven, slice and serve hot.

Chicago-style Deep Dish Pizza Dough: In a large bowl, combine the water, yeast, and sugar and stir to combine. Let's sit up until the mixture is foamy, about 5 minutes.

Add 1 1/2 cups of the flour, the semolina, 1/2 cup of the oil, and the salt, mixing by hand until it is all incorporated and the mixture is smooth. Continue adding the flour, working the dough after each addition until all the flour is incorporated but the dough is still slightly sticky. 3 to 5 minutes. Oil a large mixing bowl with remaining 2 teaspoons oil.

Place the dough in the bowl and turn to oil all sides. Cover the bowl with plastic wrap and set in a warm, draft-free place until nearly doubled in size, 1 to 1 1/2 hours.

Divide into 2 equal parts and use as directed.

Detroit-Style Pepperoni Pizzas

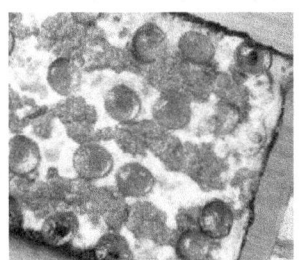

Ingredients
3 tablespoons olive oil
1 batch Pizza Dough, recipe follows
8 ounces sliced pepperoni, about 1/8 inch thick (look for small-size pepperoni sticks)
16 ounces brick cheese (or whole-milk mozzarella), cut into 1/2-inch cubes
Pizza sauce, store-bought or homemade, recipe follows
Pizza Dough:
2 1/4 cups all-purpose flour
2 teaspoons kosher salt
1 teaspoon rapid rise yeast
1 teaspoon sugar
Olive oil, for oiling the bowl
Pizza Sauce:
1 tablespoon olive oil
2 teaspoons dried Italian seasoning
2 cloves garlic, minced
One 28-ounce can crushed tomatoes
2 teaspoons sugar

Kosher salt and freshly ground black pepper

Method

Special equipment:

a Detroit-style pizza pan, optional

Position a oven rack in the bottom of the oven and preheat to the highest temperature setting, 500 to 550 degrees F.

Pour the oil in a large, square metal cake pan (or, ideally, an authentic Detroit-style pizza pan).

Put the Pizza Dough in the pan and gently stretch it out to fit so the dough reaches the corners. If the dough is being temperamental, set it for another 10 minutes to relax and try again.Later the pepperoni on the dough.

Then lay the cheese cubes all over, especially around the perimeter up to the edge of the pan (this creates the coveted crispy cheese crust). 10 o'clock 15 minutes until bubbly and golden and a crispy cheese crust has been formed. Using a fish spatula, loosen the edges and place on a cutting board. Slice into squares and serve!

Pizza Dough:

Put the flour, salt, yeast and sugar in a food processor with a metal blade attachment and pulse to combine. Add 1 cup warm water, then process until a ball forms, about 30 seconds (if a ball does not form, add a bit more flour). Process for another 30 seconds, then roll into a tight ball and place in a lightly oiled bowl. Proof in a warm spot until the dough doubles in size, about 2 hours.

Pizza Sauce:

Heat a small saucepan over medium heat and add the oil. Add the Italian seasoning and garlic and saute until the fragrance; do not let the garlic burn. Add the tomatoes and sugar and season with salt and pepper. Bring to a simmer and simmer until concentrated, about 30 minutes. Set aside to cool.

Grandma-Style Pizza

INGREDIENTS

One 28-oz.can whole peeled tomatoes

2 anchovies

2 garlic cloves

6 tablespoons olive oil

1 / 4 cup basil leaves

Salt

Pepper

12 ounces fresh mozzarella, grated

PREPARATION

Drain one 28-oz. can of whole peeled tomatoes and pulse tomatoes with 2 anchovies, 2 garlic cloves, 6 tablespoons olive oil, and 1/4 cup basil leaves in a food processor or blender until mostly smooth (some texture is okay); season with salt and pepper. Put It All Together: A classic grandma-just sauce and mozzarella-flips the usual script: Add cheese before sauce. Master this basic pie and you're ready to improvise (see below for ideas).

Classic Mozzarella Pie: Place a rack in lower third of oven and preheat to 525 ° or as high as oven will go. Once Grandma-Style Pizza Dough has risen on a baking sheet, top with 12 ounces fresh mozzarella, grated, and dot pie with 1 1 / 2 cups Fresh Tomato Pizza Sauce. Bake pie until golden brown and crisp on bottom and sides, 20-30 minutes.

Grandma-Style Pizza Dough

INGREDIENTS

1 envelope active dry yeast (about 2 1/4 teaspoons)

1 1/2 cups warm water (105-110 °)

2 tablespoons olive oil, plus 1/2 cup

2 cups all-purpose flour

2 teaspoons kosher salt

2 cups all-purpose flour

PREPARATION

Combine 1 envelope active dry yeast (about 2 1/4 teaspoons) and 1 1/2 cups warm water (105-110 °) in a large bowl; let stand until yeast starts to foam, about 10 minutes.

Mix in 2 tablespoons olive oil, then 2 cups all-purpose flour and 2 teaspoons kosher salt. Add another 2 cups all-purpose flour, a cup at a time, mixing until incorporated and a shaggy dough forms.

Turn out the dough onto a lightly floured surface and knead until soft, smooth, and elastic, 10-12 minutes.

Place dough in a lightly oiled bowl and cover with plastic wrap. Chill 24 hours.

Coat an 18x13 "rimmed baking sheet with 1/2 cup olive oil

Gently and gradually stretch the dough until it reaches the edges of the baking sheet.

Cover dough on a baking sheet tightly and with a warm place (but not too warm! is puffed and full of air bubbles, 30-40 min

New Haven-Style Clam Pizza

INGREDIENTS

1 teaspoon sugar

1 cup warm water

1/4-ounce packaging (2 1/2 teaspoons) active dry yeast

2 to 2 3/4 cups all-purpose flour

2 teaspoons salt

3 large garlic cloves, minced

1 / 4 cup olive oil

cornmeal for sprinkling baker's peel

12 littleneck clams , schucked, reserving liquor

1 teaspoon dried oregano, crumbled

2 tablespoons freshly grated Romano cheese

PREPARATION

1. In a small bowl dissolve sugar in 1/4 cup water. Sprinkle yeast over water and let stand up foamy, about 5 minutes.

2. In a large bowl stir together 2 cups flour, remaining 3/4 cup water, salt, and yeast mixture.

3. Transfer dough to a floured surface and clean and oil large bowl

.4. Knead dough vigorously, incorporating as much of remaining 3/4 cup flour as needed to create a silky dough, a full 15 minutes.

5. Transfer dough to prepared bowl, turning to coat slightly with oil, and cover bowl with 2 tight layers of plastic wrap. Let dough rise in a warm place 2 to 3 hours, or until doubled in bulk.

6. While dough is rising, in a small bowl combine the garlic and oil and chill, covered.

7. Punch down the dough and flatten on a lightly floured surface. Pounding with heel of hand and lifting, stretch dough carefully and work into a roundabout 15 inches in diameter (or into 2 smaller rounds) .

8. Put pizza stone on bottom shelf of oven and preheat oven to 500 ° F.

9. Sprinkle baker's peel with cornmeal and slide dough onto it. Cover dough with a kitchen towel and let it rest, covered with the kitchen towel, about 15 minutes. While the dough is resting, let the garlic come to room temperature.

10. Brush dough evenly with garlic oil, leaving a 1/2-inch border untouched. Arrange clams with a dash of reserved oil over oil and sprinkle with oregano and romano.

11. Shake and slide pizza off the baker's peel onto pizza stone in oven. Reduce oven temperature to 450 ° F.

and bake pizza 15 minutes, or until crust is medium brown.

12. Serve pizza immediately with plenty of napkins. Serves 2 as an entrée or 4 as a hors d'oeuvre.

New York-Style Pizza

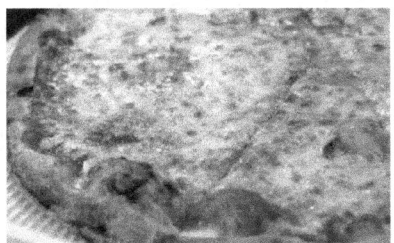

Ingredients

1 teaspoon active dry yeast

2 / 3 cup warm water (110 degrees F / 45 degrees C)

2 cups all-purpose flour

1 teaspoon salt

2 tablespoons olive oil

1 (10 ounce) can tomato sauce

1 pound shredded mozzarella cheese

1 / 2 cup grated Romano cheese

1 / 4 cup chopped fresh basil

1 tablespoon dried oregano

1 teaspoon red pepper flakes

2 tablespoons olive oil

Method

Sprinkle the yeast over the surface of the warm water in a large bowl. Let stand for 1 minute, then stir to dissolve. Mix in the flour, salt and olive oil. When the dough is too thick to stir, turn out onto a floured surface, and knead for 5 minutes. Knead in a little more flour if the dough is too sticky. Place into an oiled bowl, cover, and set aside in a warm place to rise until doubled in bulk.

Preheat the oven to 475 degrees F (245 degrees C). If using a pizza stone, preheat it in the oven as well, setting it on the lowest shelf.

When the dough has risen, flatten it out on a lightly floured surface. Roll or stretch out into a 12 inch circle, and place on a baking pan. If you are using a pizza stone, you can place it on a piece of parchment while preheating the stone in the oven.

Spread the tomato sauce evenly over the dough. Sprinkle with oregano, mozzarella cheese, basil, Romano cheese and red pepper flakes.

Bake for 12 to 15 minutes in the preheated oven, until the bottom of the crust is browned when you lift up the edge a little, and cheese is melted and bubbly . Cool for about 5 minutes before slicing and serving.

Pizza Bagels

Ingredients

bagels

shredded mozzarella cheese

tomato sauce spices (optional)

pepperoni (optional)

Step 2: Slice and Toast Bagel
Carefully cut the bagel in half and pop it into the toaster for some light toasting. This step is key if you do not want the bagel to be all soggy from your sauce when you bake it later on.

Step 3: Sauce
Spoon some tomato sauce to your bagel. I like a lot of sauce, but you must put on if much you like.

Step 4: Cheese
After the sauce comes all important cheese. Sprinkle grated mozzarella over the top of the sauce. You're just combined the holy trinity of ingredients - no, not a mixture of onions, celery and carrots known in french as a mirepoix; but bread, sauce and cheese to

form a basic pizza!
Step 5: Add Toppings
Sprinkle on some spices like powdered garlic, oregano and crushed red pepper if you want to make your pizza bagel a bit.
Finally, if you're a pepper fan, now's on add some slices.
Step 6: Bake
Set your toaster oven to bake and turn the temperature knob to 400. Then, the cheese does not make a mess inside the toaster oven and throw your pizza bagels on in there.
Step 7: Cook and Eat
Cook the pizza bagels until the cheese gets all bubbly and brown in some spots, or, until the pepperoni gets crispy.
As the baby is in the Ellio's Pizza commercial used to say, "When the cheese goes blub blub blub, it's done

St.Louis-Style Pizza

INGREDIENTS
Crustin large mixing bowl combine
 2 cups + 2 tbsp flour
1 / 2 teaspoon salt
1 teaspoon baking powder
2 teaspoons olive oil
2 teaspoons dark corn syrup
1 / 2 cup water
2 tablespoons water Sauce
16 ounces whole tomatoes (diced into fine pieces)
6 ounces tomato paste
1 1/2 tablespoons sugar
1 teaspoon crushed
1 cup 2 teaspoon salt
1/4 teaspoon salt
1 / 4 teaspoon thyme cheese shredded
1 / 2 cup provolone cheese, shredded

1 teaspoon liquid hickory liquid smoke Italian Seasoning

2 teaspoons oregano

2 teaspoons basil

PREPARATION

Crust: Mix until thoroughly combined. The dough is ready to use "as-is" No need to rise or knead. Divide the dough in half, shape into a round ball and roll out paper thin. In order to move the crusts around a pizza peel sprinkled with cornmeal works well. Sauce: Combine together and it's ready to use - do not pre-cook the sauce! Pizza pies Cheese: Toss until cheeses and smoke flavoring are completely incorporated. It's enough cheese for two (2) 12 "pizza pies. At home you'll have the best results using a pizza stone and an oven temperature around 450 degrees. If you do not have a pizza stone, use the thinnest baking sheet you have and the lowest oven rack position. The pizza is done when the underside of the crust is a dark golden brown, and the cheese has a slight golden tint to it. Underbaking the crust will result in a hard crust, resulting in a hard, tough, burn-tasting crust, getting the right baking time to produce a crisp crust will require a bit of experimentation. The amount and type of toppings you use will also affect the total baking time. A rule-of-thumb is pizza after about 10-12 minutes and adjust baking time from there therely

Neapolitan Pizza

Ingredients
For the dough:
1 1/2 cups plus 2 tablespoons warm water (100 degrees F to 110 degrees F)
3/4 teaspoon active dry yeast
4 cups unbleached all-purpose flour, plus more for dusting
2 1/2 teaspoons kosher salt
Extra-virgin olive oil, for brushing cornmeal, for dusting
For the toppings:
1 28-ounce can whole peeled tomatoes (preferably San Marzano) Kosher salt
8 ounces fresh mozzarella cheese, sliced
Extra-virgin olive oil, for drizzling
Torn fresh basil, for topping
Method
Make the dough:

Combine the warm water and yeast in a small bowl, stirring to dissolve the yeast. Combine the flour and salt in a bowl. Add the yeast mixture to the flour and stir to make a shaggy dough. (If it feels too wet and sticky, add a little water.) Transfer to a lightly oiled surface and knead until smooth and elastic, about 3 minutes. Place an inverted bowl over the dough and let rise slightly, 30 minutes. Divide the dough into 4 pieces and form each into a ball; arrange 3 inches apart on a lightly oiled baking sheet. Rub the tops of the dough lightly with olive oil and cover the baking sheet with plastic wrap. Refrigerate overnight.

Remove the dough from the refrigerator about 2 hours before baking; let sit, cover, ready to use. One hour before baking, put a pizza stone or inverted baking sheet on the middle oven rack and preheat to 500 degrees F (or 550 degrees F if your oven goes that high).

Make the sauce:

Combine the tomatoes and their juices with 1 teaspoon salt in a blender; blend until smooth.

Generously sprinkle a pizza peel or an inverted baking sheet with cornmeal. Place 1 ball of dough upside down on the cornmeal using floured hands. Gently pull the dough into an 8-to 10-inch circle, refilling your hands as needed and being careful not to deflate the dough. Spread about 1/4 cup tomato sauce on the crust; top with one-quarter of the mozzarella. Drizzle with 1 to 2 teaspoons olive oil and season with salt.

Slide the pizza onto the hot stone and bake until the crust is dark golden brown and the cheese is bubbling, 7 to 9 minutes. Transfer to a cutting board and sprinkle with basil. Let cool 2 minutes before slicing. Repeat to make 3 more pizzas.

Cook's Note

Refrigerating the dough overnight gives this crust a slightly chewy texture

Sicilian Pizza

Ingredients
For the dough:
4 cups all-purpose flour, plus more for dusting
2 teaspoons sugar
2 teaspoons kosher salt
1 teaspoon instant yeast
1 3/4 cups warm water (100 degrees F to 110 degrees F)
6 tablespoons extra-virgin olive oil, plus more for the bowl
For the toppings:
1 28-ounce can whole peeled tomatoes (preferably San Marzano)
1 1/2 teaspoons kosher salt, plus more for sprinkling
12 ounces whole milk mozzarella, thinly sliced

Method
Make the dough:
Whisk the flour, sugar, salt and the yeast in a medium bowl. Pour the warm water into a large bowl, then add the flour mixture and stir until combined. Stir in 2 tablespoons olive oil to make a very sticky dough. Turn

out onto a lightly floured surface and knead until dough comes together and no longer sticks to your finger, about 2 minutes. Transfer to a lightly oiled big bowl and turn to coat. Tightly cover with plastic wrap and refrigerate overnight.

Coat an 11-by-17-inch rimmed baking sheet with 3 tablespoons olive oil. Add the dough and stretch it to fit the baking sheet. Brush with the remaining 1 tablespoon olive oil. In the same way, place a rack in the upper third of the oven and preheat to 450 degrees F.

Make the sauce:

combine the tomatoes and their juices and the salt in a hand with your hands or a potato masher. Uncover the dough and sprinkle with salt. Gently place the baking sheet in the oven (the dough might deflate if it is knocked). Bake until golden, about 20 minutes. Remove the crust from the oven, top with the sliced mozzarella and cover with 2 cups of the crushed tomatoes. Bake until the cheese is bubbling through the sauce and starts browning, 15 to 20 more minutes.

Let the pizza stand 10 minutes, then remove from the pan using a spatula and transfer to a cutting board. Let cool 1 to 2 minutes before slicing.

Greek Pizza

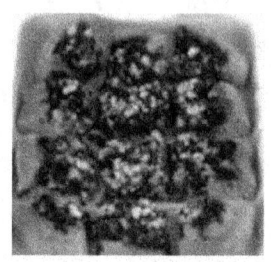

Ingredients
Crust:
Cornmeal, for dusting
Flour, for dusting
1 (1 pound) ball store-bought pizza dough
Topping:
3 tablespoons extra-virgin olive oil
2 leeks, pale green and white parts only, thinly sliced
Salt and freshly ground black pepper
3 cloves garlic, minced
12 ounces baby spinach leaves
1 (4-ounce) chunk feta cheese, crumbled (recommended: Athenos)
3/4 cup chopped fresh mint
2 tablespoons unsalted butter, softened
Method
For the crust:

Place an oven rack in the center of the oven. Preheat the oven to 450 degrees F. Dust a heavy baking sheet with cornmeal. Set aside.

On a lightly floured work surface, roll out the dough into a 1/4-inch thick rectangle about 16 inches long and 8 inches wide. Transfer the dough to the prepared baking sheet.

For the topping:

In a large skillet, heat the oil over medium-high heat. Add the leeks and season with salt and pepper. Cook, stirring frequently until tender, about 5 minutes. Add the garlic and cook for 30 seconds until aromatic. In batches, add the spinach and cook until wilted, about 5 minutes. Remove the pan from the heat and add the feta cheese and mint. Season with salt and pepper, to taste.

Using the tines of a fork, the surface of the dough all over. Spread the spinach mixture on top and dot with butter.

Bake until the dough is golden and crunchy, 15 to 18 minutes. Cut into squares and serve.

Lahm Bi Ajeen Pizza

Ingredients

250 gr white flour

salt 20 gr yeast

2 tsp sugar

3 medium Onions

3 pcs Garlic

1 bch Parsley

250 gr Lamb or beef - chopped

3 pcs Tomato

2 tsp Cumin

1 tsp paprika powder

Fresh black peppercorns - ground grease for the oven tray

Method

1. Put the flour and the tsp salt into a bowl. Mix the yeast with the flour.then add sugar and a little warm water. If it is to change to a pre-daugh with the addition of flour if needed. Keep it for 10 minutes after covering.

2. Add 2 tbsp oil and knead the dough well. Then mix it

with warm water following instructions.The dough should not be wet and should not stick to the bowl. Roll into a ball and leave in a warm place for 1hr.
3. Mix all the dough ingredients and work with your hands Until you get a firm dough. 8 inches width OR roll it to becomes a rounded flat piece with 1 cm as possible and make a border using your fingers.
4. Chop the peeled onions and press the garlic through a garlic press. Wash and finely chop parsley.
5. Put the oil in a pan and press the minced meat, onions and garlic for about 5 minutes, tomato in small pieces, pepper, salt and mix it together. take away from the heat. 5. Preheat oven to 200c.
6. Grease the baking tray, put the mankoushe on it and spread all the pizza and cook in the middle of the oven for 10-15 mins. Wait till the bread becomes golden brown.

Margherita Pizza

INGREDIENTS:

FOR PASTA

2 lb Italian "00" flour or all-purpose flour

1 oz fresh yeast

2 cups water

1 teaspoon salt

FOR DRESSING

6 tablespoons extra virgin olive oil

1 lb mozzarella cheese basil leaves to taste

1 lb canned tomatoes salt to taste

PREPARATION:

STEP 1

On a wooden or marble work surface, shape the flour into a well. Place the yeast, salt and warm water in the center. Be careful not to let the salt come in contact with the yeast.

STEP 2

Knead the dough vigorously with your hands for 15-20 minutes, or in a mixer, until the dough is soft and smooth.

STEP 3

Once you have the right consistency, adding a bit of water or flour if needed, shape the dough into a ball. Cover with a plastic bowl so that the dough is protected from the air. Let rise for 3 or 4 hours at room temperature for about an hour in a warm place.

STEP 4

Once the dough will be doubled in volume, the six loaves, in the spherical shapes, cover with a sheet of plastic wrap and let them rise at room temperature for a couple of hours or in a warm place for about 45 minutes.

STEP 5

As soon as the loaves have doubled in volume, prepare the tomato sauce and place it in a bowl. Add a pinch of salt and 1/3 of the olive oil.

STEP 6

Knead the dough, then flattening them using your fingers.

STEP 7

Use a ladle or a spoon to spread a good amount of tomato sauce on the pizza. Then, cover with mozzarella, torn into pieces. Garnish with a couple of leaves of basil and bake in a 480 ° F oven for 5 or 6 minutes.

STEP 8

Once ready, remove the pizza from the oven. Garnish with more basil and a drizzle of oil. Serve immediately.

Marinara Pizza

Pizza Dough
INGREDIENTS
3/4 cup warm water (105 ° -115 ° F) 1
1/2 teaspoons active dry yeast
2 cups unbleached all-purpose flour
1 teaspoon salt
PREPARATION
In a measuring cup stir together water and yeast until yeast is dissolved. In a large bowl whisk together flour and salt and add yeast mixture, stirring until a soft dough forms. On a lightly floured surface knead dough until smooth and elastic, about 10 minutes. Oil a large bowl (preferably with olive oil) and transfer dough to bowl, turning to coat. Cover bowl with plastic wrap. Let's dough rise in a warm place until doubled in bulk, about 1 1/2 hours. On a lightly floured surface flatten dough with your hands. Cut the dough in half and form into 2 balls. (Dough may be made 1 day forward to this point). Dust tops of the flour and cover each ball with an inverted bowl large enough to allow dough to

expand. Let dough rise in a warm place until doubled in bulk, about 1 hour.

www.ingramcontent.com/pod-product-compliance
Lightning Source LLC
Chambersburg PA
CBHW071438070526
44578CB00001B/124